MW00675749

"I wanted to see how I could dismantle language and sound so that they would become exciting again."

Jeff Tweedy, p. 83

Contents

NO DEPRESSION

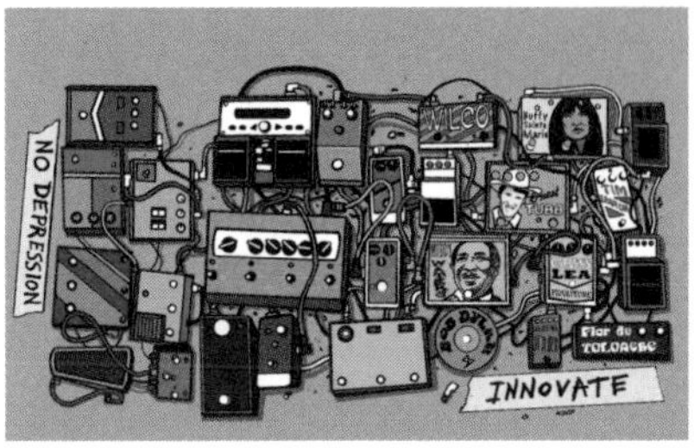

ON THE COVER

The cover of the "Innovate" issue shows a web of effects pedals looped and linked together. Literally, these tools create a range of different sounds, which allow musicians to explore new, innovative ideas with their work. Metaphorically, though, muralist and percussionist Scott Nurkin — who is also featured in the journal (page 104) — used this imagery to represent the interconnectivity of innovations that change the way we make and consume roots music.

Inside covers: Lyrics from Carrie Jacobs-Bond's "A Perfect Day." Illustrations by Drew Christie.

NO DEPRESSION TEAM
Chris Wadsworth *Publisher*
Hilary Saunders *Managing Editor*
Stacy Chandler *Assistant Editor*
Sonja Nelson *Advertising*
Adam Kirr *Social Media Manager*
Henry Carrigan *Print Partnerships*
Maureen Cross *Finance/Operations*

WEB nodepression.com
TWITTER & INSTAGRAM @nodepression
FACEBOOK facebook.com/nodepressionmag

GENERAL INQUIRIES
info@nodepression.com

ONLINE ADVERTISING
advertising@nodepression.com

SUBSCRIPTIONS
store.nodepression.com

JOURNAL DESIGN & PRODUCTION
Marcus Amaker

Printed in Nashville, Tennessee, by Lithographics Inc.

No Depression is part of the FreshGrass Foundation.
freshgrass.org

ISBN-13: 978-0-9994674-5-9

Hello Stranger

BY HILARY SAUNDERS

Innovation is messy business. It's complicated and tangled like the tubes on this issue's cover, illustrated by musician and muralist Scott Nurkin.

Brilliant, perfect ideas don't just spring fully formed from an innovator's mind, like the Greek myth of Athena leaping to life out of Zeus' forehead. (Well, there is that one real-life legend about how "Yesterday" came to The Beatles' Paul McCartney in his sleep and then he woke up and wrote the classic ballad note for note, but let's all acknowledge that as an exception.)

Instead, innovations take time and many revisions. But when they arrive, they change the course of society and culture. It's readily apparent in music, where innovations have altered the way we make, consume, listen to, and experience songs, albums, and live performances.

Even when we at *No Depression* came up with this theme for the Fall-Winter 2018 issue, the terminology went through some edits. At first, we thought the title "Innovators and Innovations" would fit, highlighting the scope of creators and the creations we've covered. However, as the journal came together, we realized that in addition to the people and products, there's another piece to this puzzle — the process of innovating.

As a result, we're calling this issue "Innovate." It's a verb, an action, and an exclamation. The word "innovate" invokes a sense of excitement and mystery, something that makes us take stock of the current state of roots music and consider what else can be done.

KRISTINA MORAVEC

This issue is more about how innovators create and how their innovations affect those around us than rehashing the most famous innovations in roots music. Our goal was not to retell innovators' origin stories or regurgitate the canon. Rather, we strove to find and share tales that haven't been told before — of technological developments that are on the cusp of breaking boundaries, of unsung heroes who have built careers on the differences that make them unique, and of new methods of making a living as a roots musician in the 21st century.

Inside these pages, we examine the role of instruments like the parlor piano and dreadnought guitar and how they affected the earliest sounds of roots music. We also look at how a new bowing technique on stringed instruments upset the status quo. In terms of broader cultural movements, we dive into subgenres of roots music like cowpunk and outlaw country, investigating how these styles upended their predecessors. Technologically speaking, we explore the looping effects utilized by Wilco and Gaelynn Lea, and how Jeremy Dutcher transformed Native Canadian music from century-old wax cylinders into digitized and original works.

On a personal note, there's a story my family likes to tell about how I've always been averse to messes. Apparently when I was in preschool, my class took a field trip that had all of us walking in the mud. As soon as my light-up sneakers touched the wet and slimy earth, I unleashed that blood-curdling, baby dinosaur-like yowl of an unhappy 2-year-old. Thanks to a sense of obstinacy (that I may or may not still retain) and a deep reluctance to get dirty, I made my poor preschool teacher carry me the rest of the day.

These days the mud is more metaphorical, but like many other writers, I still get scared when starting new projects because I'm afraid to get messy. The first draft will never be perfect; it'll always be kind of a mess because the process of creating is never linear. So, kick the mud off your shoes (or let it cake on there, we don't judge!) and take a gander as we dig into the messy means of innovators, innovations, and innovating in the Fall-Winter 2018 issue of *No Depression.*

MUSIC FOR THE MASSES

The parlor piano's role in American songwriting

by Kim Ruehl

WHEN CARRIE JACOBS married Dr. Frank Lewis Bond in 1888, she was 26 years old with a son from her first marriage. While conventions of the day expected her to keep the home and tend to the child, Frank and Carrie had been close since their youth and he was happy to help her explore her interests in ceramics, piano, and music composition.

The couple moved to Michigan, nearly 300 miles north of their hometown of Janesville, Wisconsin. While Frank found work, the pay was nothing impressive. Carrie's extra income from selling her ceramics and offering piano lessons was welcome.

It was barely two decades past the end of the Civil War, and Jacobs-Bond — she hyphenated her last name to honor Frank — was among the first generation of Americans who had grown up with a piano in the house. In the century since the upright piano was first introduced in Italy, around the dawn of the American Revolution and in the heyday of Wolfgang Amadeus Mozart, the instrument had gone from a plaything for wealthy elites to something that was beginning to be manufactured for and marketed to the growing American middle class.

Before the upright, or parlor piano, music was something many people had to leave their homes to experience. Much of the beloved music of the day was composed by Europeans and bankrolled by monarchies. When Carrie Jacobs-Bond was a little girl, Europe teemed with Romantic Era composers — Johann Strauss, Franz Liszt, Robert Schumann — who flipped the role of music in society on its head as they explored how traditional folk melodies could be revitalized on the piano through their compositions. Despite his boy band-level fame, for example, Liszt explored folk music in much the same way as Bob Dylan and his contemporaries would a century later.

As Jacobs-Bond grew in her childhood piano lessons, though, she got to experience an advance in music technology whose impact was akin to that today of Spotify. The spread of parlor pianos in middle class homes leading up to, and especially after the Civil War, meant that music composed by the greats was suddenly available for purchase via sheet music. No longer was music performance only in the hands of professionals; the fledgling music industry proliferated sheet music for performance by the common person, and the middle class lapped it up. Jacobs-Bond was so enamored of the possibilities inherent in selling one's music on paper that she developed an interest in writing her own music instead of just teaching people how to play the compositions of others. Like generations of folk and pop songwriters to follow, she used the act of learning other people's songs to move slowly into creating her own, and by the time she married Frank Bond, she was a gifted, intuitive songwriter.

As the 20th century dawned, though, women were not recognized as legitimate in the world of music composition, a fact Jacobs-Bond more or less took for granted. She composed on the side once her regular daily duties were done.

Then, one morning when Frank was out walking in the snow, he passed by a few children having a snowball fight. One of their powder-packed projectiles struck him in such a way that he lost his balance and fell on the ice, cracking a rib. A few days later, he died from the injury.

Shocked, grief-stricken, Jacobs-Bond moved back to Janesville, took in a boarder, and started selling furniture to cover her expenses. Through word of mouth, she managed to pick up a little extra cash for her compositions and was so encouraged that she and her son, Frederick, moved to Chicago to be closer to music publishers. None of them would have her, of course, so Jacobs-Bond created her own publishing company and began printing her music herself. Thus, two centuries before Ani DiFranco blazed a trail as a wholly independent artist via Righteous Babe Records, Carrie Jacobs-Bond was America's original indie songwriter, with every penny from her sentimental, lyric-driven parlor music going straight into her pocket.

PHOTO COURTESY OF ROCK COUNTY HISTORICAL SOCIETY

Ragtime pianist Max Morath, in conversation with National Public Radio in 2009, noted that Jacobs-Bond "had a relentless ego. Now, you know something? We would say that about George Gershwin, and we'd say it about Irving Berlin. And we'd say it about any male composer. Of course they have overwhelming egos. Of course they want success. Of course they try to handle their public image. Carrie Jacobs-Bond never had a press agent. She was her [own] best press agent."

And while she was a feminist and generally a daring woman, she was well aware of the appropriate topics in songwriting of the day. She adhered to the conventions to make a name for herself, which was more than enough for her.

As the years passed, many popular singers picked up her material, appreciating her moxie and determined to keep her legacy alive. One of her greatest compositions, "Just A-Wearyin' for You," recorded by the folksinger and actor Paul Robeson, carries echoes of the folk songs of Scottish poet Robert Burns, whose vision of a popular music for the common people was about a century ahead of its time.

"Morning comes, the birds awake
Seem to sing so for your sake
But there's sadness in the notes
That come trillin' from their throats
Seem to feel a sadness too
Just a-wearyin' for you"

With songs such as that, and "I Love You Truly," "A Perfect Day," and "We Are All Americans," Jacobs-Bond became one of the best-selling songwriters in American history. She self-published 174 songs and sold more than one million copies of sheet music for "I Love You Truly" alone. Though she died from a heart attack in 1946, she was posthumously inducted into the Songwriters Hall of Fame in 1970, the same year as other, now better-known American songwriters like Woody Guthrie, Lead Belly, and Francis Scott Key.

The American Songbook

Of course, Jacobs-Bond was not the first parlor songwriter, and she has certainly not proven the most celebrated. That would be Stephen Foster, who predated Jacobs-Bond, is often called the Father of American Music, and composed more than 200 pieces in his lifetime.

Foster, a child of antebellum America who only visited the South once, was a champion of the woefully racist practice of minstrelsy. His parlor songs — "Oh! Susanna," "Old Folks at Home," "Old Black Joe," "Camptown Races" — have become staples, with select verses introduced to children during elementary school.

Born on the Fourth of July in 1826 in Pennsylvania, Foster was the youngest of 10 children in a well-off family that could afford a parlor piano before many others. His father served in the Pennsylvania State Legislature and was, for a time, the mayor of a small town outside of Pittsburgh.

Foster had only one formal music teacher in his life, Henry Kleber, but taught himself music via his explorations of various instruments, including the piano. As was true of many parlor music composers, Foster pulled from a number of traditions, preferring to write in the common vernacular instead of the foreign languages preferred by the symphonic composers who were his contemporaries. According to the Library of Congress, "Foster displayed an affinity for 'Ethiopian' and minstrel songs (he performed in minstrel shows as a boy), yet he also incorporated characteristics of Irish melodies, German songs, and Italian operas in his compositions."

His affection for minstrelsy — a common subgenre of parlor music — has proven to be one of the most unfortunate facts of Foster's biography, since he contributed so many beloved melodies and verses to the American songbook.

During its time, minstrelsy was common and reflected the oppressive racist views of much of white America. After the Civil War, it eventually proved anathema, as more Americans became acquainted with actual people of color, instead of the caricatures that were presented in the minstrel program. That Foster wrote in an exaggerated version of ebonics and liberally employed the n-word does not stand up under today's scrutiny and does not support any view of him being at all enlightened as a master of cultural expression. During his time, however, it would have been radical for him to tackle this style of songwriting in any other way, and he was not a radical man. Thus, holding up his legacy requires contemporary scholars and listeners to reckon with the undesirable truths about America's past. As with much of the country's complex, sometimes unfortunate history, a few things are true at once: "Oh! Susanna" employs one of America's best-written melodies by one of its most intuitive songwriters, and its verses are incredibly racist.

It's easy to imagine that Jacobs-Bond was influenced in some way by Foster's smooth-flowing melodies. Sentimentality and white nostalgia were typical themes of the day's popular music, though it says much about the culture of the time that Foster's racist verses were acceptable but it would have been terribly offensive for Jacobs-Bond to veer from the standard female topics of romantic love and general emotionalism.

At any rate, Foster began writing songs at a young age — he was 14 when he first published in 1840, two decades before the Civil War began. But it wasn't until he moved to Cincinnati and began working as a bookkeeper at his brother's steamboat company that he truly began to flourish as a songwriter.

At that time, according to his biography in the Songwriters Hall of Fame, "Cincinnati society was a convergence of the Industrial working class, Irish, English and Scottish aristocracy, plantation slaves, and river life. Foster soon abandoned the pursuit of business and dedicated himself to writing songs inspired by the cultures that surrounded him. In 1848, he sold 'Oh! Susanna' and 'Old Uncle Ned' to W.C. Peters and in 1849 negotiated a contract with New York publishers Firth & Pond Co." Thus, as America tumbled toward a civil war, it was with minstrel shows on the stage, more and more pianos in the parlor, and the songs of Stephen Foster on everyone's lips.

From Drippy to Zippy

There were plenty of other parlor music composers of great note as the 19th century gave way to the 20th. New York City's society of songwriters and publishers during the parlor piano heyday was famously called Tin Pan Alley, a scene that sprung up around 28th Street in Manhattan somewhere between the peak of Foster's career and the beginning of Jacobs-Bond's. Its most celebrated artists include Irving Berlin and Scott Joplin, the Gershwin brothers — Ira and George — as well as Cole Porter and other innovators who transformed the parlor music trend from drippy, sappy songs to something more zippy, paving the way for the jazz and blues performers who dominated between the world wars. And while some folk purists would shy away from recognizing Tin Pan Alley as part of the diaspora of American roots music, the tunes of the American Songbook are as inextricably American as is, say, "This Land Is Your Land" — a song which, incidentally, was inspired by Tin Pan Alley composer Irving Berlin's "God Bless America." (Woody Guthrie's original refrain was somewhat of a middle finger to Berlin's song, which claimed "God blessed America for me.")

Over the years, Tin Pan Alley went from a group of publishers focused on proliferating sheet music to supplying vaudeville performances with fresh material and, eventually, songwriting for the next big thing — recorded music.

"Technologies are associated with habits, sometimes crystallizing them and sometimes enabling them," writes Jonathan Sterne in *The Audible Past: Cultural Origins of Sound Recording.* "... Our most cherished pieties about sound-reproduction technologies — for instance, that they separated sounds from their sources or that sound recording allows us to hear the voices of the dead — were not and are not innocent empirical descriptions of the technologies' impact. They were wishes that people grafted onto sound-reproduction technologies — wishes that became programs for innovation and use."

Indeed, the idea for recording sound had been around for quite a while, even well before it became a reality. There was an idea that recording could serve educational and scientific interests, could assist deaf people, or could help provide spiritual insight by allowing people to record the final thoughts of their dying relatives. There was no way to predict how central sound recording would become in the world of music, but with the intertwining of music with American life, it was also perhaps no surprise that that would be one big use of the technology.

Thomas Edison's phonograph was introduced in 1877, 13 years after Stephen Foster's death. And while it was a groundbreaking invention, it took about another half-century for recorded music to surpass sheet music in the hearts and homes of the average American.

Nowadays, with technology changing at such a breakneck pace, with new methods for music delivery popping into the marketplace almost annually, it's hard to imagine how such a pivotal piece of technology managed to dance around as a novelty instead of

Just Awearyin' For You

from
Seven Songs

As unpretentious as the Wild Rose

Carrie Jacobs-Bond

Published at
THE BOND SHOP
BY
CARRIE JACOBS-BOND & SON
INCORPORATED
746 SO. MICHIGAN AVE.
CHICAGO

*High
Low

PRICE 60 CENTS
2/—Net

THE FREDERICK HARRIS CO.
Authorized Agents for the British Empire
49 QUEEN STREET EAST, TORONTO, CANADA
89 NEWMAN STREET WEST, LONDON, ENGLAND

a daily habit for so long. This teaches us something about the relationship so many Americans had with music at the time.

Sure, music performances continued to draw audiences and there were professional musicians who captured the attention and imagination of the country. But the average person, on a day-to-day basis, preferred to interact with music by playing it themselves, or by listening to a performance by someone they knew and loved, right there in the living room. It wasn't until the first world war had been fought that record players really started to proliferate. Jacobs-Bond published "I Love You Truly" in 1901, eventually selling a million copies; it wasn't until 1920 that a recorded song — "Crazy Blues" by Mamie Smith — achieved the same sales landmark.

According to the Smithsonian, the phonograph was presented as a novelty experience at first: Shopkeepers would put one out on the street and passersby could slip in a coin to listen to recorded jokes, singing, stories, or even a recording of people just laughing. This sort of circus introduction to phonography was akin to a customer picking up an iPhone at the Apple store and playing with it before they buy. But there was more going on in the cultural shift over that half-century than just people toying with a new gadget.

Recording fundamentally changed the experience of both creating music and experiencing it. Before recording, the European composers as well as the American parlor songwriters like Foster, Jacobs-Bond, and Berlin were free, in a sense, in their creations. There was no limitation on how long a song could be. It was up to the artist to decide how a song began and where and when it ended. Recorded music changed that: In order for a piece of music to fit entirely on a record, it could be no longer than two to three minutes in length. Thus, when recorded music took over the music publishing world, a songwriter had to limit their artistic statement — or find a way to cram it all in there — in order to sell units and get paid.

Another fundamental change with recording was that the listener could hear someone like Scott Joplin play a song whenever they wanted to, without having to pay for a ticket time and again, and rather than listening to their sister or grandfather play it. Further, without having the musician physically in the room when the music was taking place, it created a mythos around the artist that equated them with something almost magical, rather than just another human with a remarkable skill. This transformed the medium from a fun way to connect with family and friends as people passed the time to a sort of escapist experience into which one was led by someone they would likely never even meet.

Mark Katz, in his book *Capturing Sound: How Technology Has Changed Music*, writes, "There have always been composer-performers — artists who interpret their own works — but with recording we can conceive of listener-performers and listener-composers. Recording thus not only affects the practice of music, it shapes the very way in which we *think* about music: what it is, can be, and should be."

Listening to a piece of recorded music, then, allowed people to separate from the present moment, to daydream, to imagine themselves being capable of creating such a thing — or creating something else altogether. It helped light the wick of American innovation, as the average person was able to bring into their home tangible proof of how humans can surmount the impossible — have a musician performing in the room without that musician being physically present.

There was certainly something lost when music took that leap from being a moment we participated in together, habitually, in our homes, to becoming a product that we consumed. In a way it separated us from the workaday habit of creative expression, allowing us to tell ourselves that only certain people possess that kind of creativity, and then creating a society in which that could become true. In another way it opened our imaginations to new possibilities, giving us license to pause and reflect as we listen to the brilliant performances of highly trained musicians.

To that end, Katz adds, "The fact that the phonograph was once at the center of efforts to enrich American musical life reveals less about the machine itself than it reflects contemporary attitudes about music, technology, morality, culture, education, class, race, and gender. Early phonograph ads were right when they touted the device as a mirror: a mirror, yes, not simply of sound but of society."

And that mirror is something that generations of musicians and artists in general have in common. It was King Lear's fool who carried a mirror, demonstrating one of the most vital roles of the artist in society — to stand drenched from the same rain that soaked the king, and then to lift the mirror, to show the more powerful person their own flawed humanity. The arts, like technology, are humankind's greatest democratizing force. And music technology has done this for us time and again, as recording technology has progressed from wax cylinders to vinyl records, cassette tapes, compact discs, and megabytes. But there has been perhaps no more pervasive and long-lasting technology than the drawing of notes and staffs on paper. After all, 200 hundred years after Stephen Foster, students and budding songwriters around the world still begin their musical journeys that same old way — by picking up a piece of sheet music and sitting down at a piano to play. ■

PATRICK SHEEHAN

THE BANJO KILLER

How the dreadnought acoustic guitar rang in a new era of American music

by Greg Cahill

Shawn Camp of The Earls of Leicester

THE AFTERNOON WAS HOT and humid on August 15, 1969. Under a clear blue sky, a couple hundred thousand college kids and hippies sat shoulder-to-shoulder on a hillside on 600 acres of Max Yasgur's bucolic farm in Bethel, New York, waiting to be entertained. Concertgoers poured in, many of them buzzed on warm beer, cheap wine, weed, and who knows what else.

On this opening day of the Aquarian Music and Arts Fair at Woodstock, folk star Richie Havens — flanked by guitarist Paul "Deano" Williams and conga player Daniel Ben Zebulon — took his place center stage on a plain wooden stool. Havens had been scheduled to perform fifth in the lineup, but gridlocked traffic on the adjacent two-lane blacktop had delayed most of the acts, and festival organizer Michael Lang begged Havens to open the show. He had expected to play 20 minutes; he played more than two hours. Six encores later, Havens had run through every song he knew and Lang was signaling from the wings for more.

Dressed in a saffron-colored kaftan, white cotton pants, and sandals, his back soaked with sweat, and cradling a big Guild D-40 dreadnought acoustic guitar, Havens called to the soundman for more volume on the guitar mic. His dreadnought-style guitar had a reputation as a workhorse. It was tuned to an open-D chord, accenting its deep bass notes and ringing highs. Havens wrapped the long thumb of his left hand over the fretboard and started strumming. His right hand, weighted by two large silver-and-turquoise rings, flailed over the steel strings, the guitar pick becoming a blur as he drove the rhythm, faster and faster, harder and harder. "Free-dom ... free-dom ... ," Havens chanted in his rich baritone, as he improvised a song built around the old blues spiritual "Motherless Child."

That historic performance of "Freedom" — now considered one of the greatest concert performances in folk history — was captured on the 1970 film *Woodstock*. It was a dazzling display, not only of Havens' talent and stage prowess, but also of the sonic punch that could be delivered by a dreadnought; no other guitar model could have delivered that volume or endured Havens' vigorous strumming.

A Ubiquitous Sound

The dreadnought was a major technological development in the music industry, a handcrafted marvel of American ingenuity. Invented just more than a century ago by luthiers at C.F. Martin & Co., the six- and 12-string dreadnought-style acoustic guitar was designed with an exceptionally big body that gives players more volume and cannon-shot bass, as well as clarity, to meet the demands of the changing music scene. The instrument took its name from the H.M.S. Dreadnought, a mighty British battleship launched in 1906 — its moniker meaning "fear nothing" in old English. C.F. Martin called the instrument his "big gun." Decades later, the guitar was dubbed "the banjo killer" for its ability to compete sonically with the percussive highs produced by banjos used in hillbilly music, Dixieland, and bluegrass. It has inspired countless musicians and shaped the sound of traditional music right up to today.

The dreadnought body style remains the most popular guitar sold worldwide, despite a renewed interest in parlor guitars and other small-bodied models sought by players in search of ergonomic instruments and sweet midrange tones. Martin CEO Chris Martin IV calls the dreadnought the company's "bread and butter," and it has been copied throughout the industry. Over the past few decades, Gibson Guitars and the Guild Guitar Co. have produced their own dreadnought models called jumbos. Other guitar manufacturers offer variations on the dreadnought design as well.

Since its inception, the dreadnought has played a singular role in shaping the sound of American roots music.

PATRICK SHEEHAN

Joey Ryan of The Milk Carton Kids

Country, folk, blues, Cajun, bluegrass, rock, and pop artists — from Gene Autry and Hank Williams to Doc Watson and Peter Rowan, from Johnny Cash and Elvis Presley to Jerry Garcia and Kurt Cobain, from Bob Dylan and Joni Mitchell to Keb' Mo' and John Fahey (who reportedly smashed his celebrated 1939 Recording King during a lover's quarrel) — have included dreadnoughts in their arsenal, as did The Beatles, The Rolling Stones, and Led Zeppelin. The dreadnought was a staple during the 1960s folk revival. The rise of the singer-songwriter and soft-rock eras in the early 1970s found dreadnoughts in the hands of Jackson Browne, Loggins and Messina, and Seals & Crofts.

Today, country and Americana artists such as Dwight Yoakam, Kasey Musgraves, Steve Earle, Sara Watkins, Jeff Tweedy, Jason Isbell, Mumford & Sons, Ani DiFranco, The Avett Brothers, Robbie Fulks, Sarah Jarosz, and Neko Case are among those who rely on dreadnoughts in their act. Emmylou Harris maintains a large collection of Gibson J-200 jumbo models. Shawn Camp of The Earls of Leicester uses a '39 Martin D-28 herringbone model just like the one his hero Lester Flatt played as one of Bill Monroe's Blue Grass Boys. Joey Ryan of The Milk Carton Kids plays a rare 1951 Gibson J-45, his dream guitar and a gift from a devoted fan.

There is considerable lore built around these big-bodied instruments: Folk icon Ramblin' Jack Elliott plays a Martin D-28 handpainted with a now-headless bull rider (the result of an unfortunate encounter with a spilled shot of tequila that washed away the head, he says). Iowa singer-songwriter Greg Brown is partial to the Gibson J-45 jumbo and owns a Jubal J-45 knockoff constructed by late Michigan luthier and former Gibson employee Aaron Cowles from old-growth mahogany salvaged from the loading-dock ramp of the original Gibson factory in Kalamazoo. Neil Young owns Hank Williams' 1941 D-28, which inspired the singer-songwriter's nostalgic tribute

MEGAN BAKER

"This Old Guitar." (The dreadnought is an essential part of the signature Crosby, Stills, Nash & Young sound.)

And a Martin D-28 inspired a song that became an Americana touchstone: Robbie Robertson was stuck for an opening line to "The Weight," from The Band's 1968 debut *Music from Big Pink,* until he noticed that the guitar's back center-brace stamp was branded with "C.F. Martin & Co, Nazareth, PA." After that, the lyrics began to flow easily: "I pulled into Nazareth, I was feeling 'bout half past dead."

The evocative song, with its cryptic spirituality and rustic overtones, provided a portal back to traditional music. As author Greil Marcus observed in *Ranters & Crowd Pleasers*, " ... [M]any young Americans had spent the years preceding ... *Music from Big Pink* teaching themselves to feel like exiles in their own country, and ... The Band's music, fashioned out of old styles, out of what had endured, was made as a way back into it."

The Hawaiian Connection

These days, acoustic guitars are commonplace, but it hasn't always been that way. According to the 2016 edition of *The Martin Journal*, "In the years leading up to — and in the early decades of the 20th century — the guitar was played primarily by women in high society, the well-to-do living in East Coast cities or in Chicago or Los Angeles. Called 'parlor guitars,' they were played where they could be heard: In the intimate surroundings of sitting rooms where guests gathered to be entertained. President Andrew Jackson's wife, Rachel, famously played the guitar in the White House."

The Martin dreadnought changed that and, in the process, altered American culture. "There is no other branded-specific acoustic-instrument design that has had such a far-reaching impact on the development of popular musical expression in America — and, by extension, the world," Greg Reish, director of the Center for Popular Music at Middle Tennessee State University in Murfreesboro, told *The Martin Journal*.

But while it is closely identified with traditional American music, the dreadnought's origin lies not in the smoky hollers of the Blue Ridge Mountains or the muddy fields of the Mississippi Delta, but on the cosmopolitan streets of San Francisco and on the verdant islands of Hawaii. The 1915 Panama-Pacific International Exposition in San Francisco was held to announce to the world that the City by the Bay had recovered from the devastating 1906 earthquake. One of its biggest attractions was the palatial Hawaiian pavilion — Hawaii had become a US territory just 15 years earlier and an estimated one million visitors flocked to the pavilion, built by a Hawaiian business association for a hefty $100,000 (the equivalent of $2.4 million in 2018). That grand building introduced ukuleles and Hawaiian music to eager American audiences drawn by the island's hula dancers, haunting music, colorful costumes, and exotic food.

The Royal Hawaiian Band, led by guitarist "Major" Mekia Kealaka'i, held court at the pavilion. Kealaka'i played a Hawaiian slide guitar set up with the steel strings high off the neck. "It was a big band and it played Hawaiian music unlike anything Americans had ever heard before," says historian and former Martin Guitars archivist Dick Boak. "For some reason, it caught hold with the American public and Hawaiian music spread like wildfire."

After the expo, Kealaka'i began touring vaudeville houses across the country with the stripped-down Royal Hawaiian Sextette. "However, Major Kealaka'i found that his smaller-bodied guitars could not be heard adequately by the large audiences the band drew to its increasingly popular performances," Boak says. "So, in 1916, he approached the Ditson retail-store chain, which sold Martin Guitars under its own brand name, to build a larger guitar."

Within six months, the staff at Ditson and the makers at Martin "put their heads together and came up with the dreadnought shape that we know today — the pear shape, but in the 12-fret format," Boak says. "Ditson started ordering those from Martin and offering them for sale. They weren't tremendously popular, though they were offered in a couple of different configurations. But *that* was the beginning. They were mostly all made for the Hawaiian style of playing. It seemed to fit the bill."

The music industry soon recognized that Martin had created something useful for the burgeoning phonograph and concert industries. The August 19, 1916, edition of *Music Trade Review* noted the innovative instrument had been "found to be excellent for [the] making of talking-machine records ... It is also said to be an excellent instrument for use in auditoriums and large halls." Still, at first, sales were slow: Only 30 were sold during the first 15 years, as other models like parlor guitars or smaller-bodied ones were played more often at the time. "It was not a tremendously popular model," Boak says. "Yet, when Ditson closed its doors in 1931, the dreadnought was the only one of its guitar models that Martin chose to continue."

Matinee Idols and a Bluegrass Icon

Demand for dreadnoughts grew throughout the 1930s, thanks to the rapid growth of the recording and radio industries, innovations in microphone technology, and the complementary tonal qualities of the instruments themselves. Country acts, especially cowboy musicians, readily embraced the instrument. Hollywood's most popular singing cowboy, Gene Autry, appeared larger than life on movie screens in just about every town in America, seated on a dark sorrel named Champion the Wonder Horse and clad in ornate gabardine Western wear. Taking advantage of advances in film-sound technology, onscreen he played a Martin D-45 dreadnought (first built for Autry in 1933) as he crooned "Back in the Saddle," "Tumbling Tumbleweeds," and other popular cowboy songs. "He made a big impression," Boak says. "The singing cowboy movies did a tremendous amount to extend the popularity of the dreadnought and to make people want them."

On the fledgling bluegrass scene, the dreadnought showed that it could hold its own against loud banjos and fiddles. It became common to see a group of acoustic players, including a guitarist with a dreadnought in hand, huddled around a single mic as they played. The dreadnought soon took its place alongside such iconic bluegrass instruments as the fiddle, the Mastertone banjo, and the Gibson F-5 mandolin.

The advent of bluegrass, introduced in 1939 by Kentucky-born mandolinist Bill Monroe and His Blue Grass Boys, solidified the role of the dreadnought in traditional music, especially with the development of lightning-fast flatpicked guitar licks. Monroe had purchased a 1939 Martin D-28 with herringbone trim, Sitka spruce top, and Brazilian rosewood back and sides — the quintessential prewar dreadnought. Monroe became so enthralled by its rich tone that he insisted each guitarist featured in the band — including Lester Flatt, Carter Stanley, Del McCoury, Jimmy Martin, and Peter Rowan, to name a few — play that specific instrument. Monroe reportedly even required that the guitar be used on the band's recordings, though some dispute that lore. His D-28 can be heard on the WSM-AM radio transcription of Monroe's 1939 debut at the Grand Ole Opry, on which the Blue Grass Boys performed "The Muleskinner Blues" with Monroe making a rare appearance on guitar.

Nearly 50 guitarists played Monroe's mythic guitar before it was lost to history. The last was Rowan, a Blue Grass Boy from 1963 to 1967. "Jimmy Maynard was playing guitar with Bill when I arrived in Nashville, and that was the story, that was the guitar," says Rowan, adding that the iconic '39 Martin was the guitar on which he and Monroe co-wrote and recorded the bluegrass classic "Walls of Time."

"At first I was playing my own guitar, a 1950s D-28 — nothing super special," Rowan says. "He suggested I play [his 1939 model]. He brought the guitar backstage at the Opry and suggested that I play it. I had it worked on because the action [the height of the strings] was impossible to play — it wasn't in good shape."

Then, one night in 1966, between shows at the Opry, a fellow band member drove Rowan to nearby Printer's Alley in Nashville on an errand. Someone stole Monroe's coveted Martin D-28 from the parked car. Later that night, Rowan told Monroe of the theft. "We were going backstage at the Opry," says Rowan in a somber tone. "We were standing on the back stairs — the fated back stairs where Hank Williams was told never to come back to the Opry [because of his drunkenness], where Bill told Elvis that he believed in him. That was Bill's pulpit. Those stone steps on the back of the Ryman Auditorium are still there. I remember we were standing in the doorway and he, uh, well, I thought he was going to fire me right there. He got pretty angry. It was not a happy moment."

A few elements made that particular Martin D-28 so special to Monroe. As Rowan says, "That guitar had a resonance that was a match for the sound he liked with his mandolin. ... He said that one set up the other one. Carter Stanley had played that instrument, which meant that it had the mojo. I felt exalted and honored to be able to play it. Not only because of its mythology, but also because it was built on the old Martin standards with hide glue and nitrocellulose finish. Though there wasn't much finish on it, I can tell you that. It was called the Red Guitar. It was just so old and had been left out on the trunk of the car and it had been rained on and that's why it was so great. In terms of its tone, clarity was one of its strong points. It had a sort of deep roar and real punchy bass notes. It had incredible resonance that complemented his mandolin backbeat stroke, what they call 'the chop.' There was a blend there that was unique to those two instruments. That was his iconic guitar sound."

Modern Day Mojo

The power and tonal palette of the dreadnought continues to resonate with contemporary bluegrass, progressive country, and newgrass players. You can hear it in the way a dreadnought drives the propulsive sound of Old Crow Medicine Show's latest album, *Volunteer*; on the high-lonesome newgrass of Billy Strings' *Turmoil & Tinfoil*; in the gentle strains of "Thank You, John Steinbeck," from Trampled by Turtles' *Life Is Good on the Open Road*; and in the country comfort of Jason Isbell's "Chaos and Clothes."

"The dreadnought has the quintessential bluegrass sound. It's not as mellow and mid-rangy as a smaller-bodied guitar," says bluegrass phenom Molly Tuttle. "It's solid and punchy enough to cut through a bluegrass band and bring the hard-edged tone that pervades the bluegrass genre."

And it's versatile enough to accommodate a bluegrass player with a penchant for jazz and improvisation. "The dread was always 'the sound' of a guitar associated with what was formative acoustic music to me," says the eclectic Grant Gordy, former guitarist with the David Grisman Quintet. "Some of my first musical memories revolve around Doc [Watson] and Tony Rice, particularly 'Cold on the Shoulder.' Later I discovered the Grisman Quintet and Bryan Sutton and Clarence [White] and [David] Grier and all these folks, and what did they all have in common, guitaristically? It was the undisputed standard bluegrass-ish sound.

"When in the David Grisman Quintet I had an occasion or two to play David's '39 [Martin] D-18. I remember thinking, 'Good Lord, this is the best guitar I've ever played.' Probably still is. It was somewhat revelatory and it turned me on to the idea of old guitars. They have a mojo. I've heard it's something about the way the resins in the wood crystalize over time, but I don't really know. Subtle overtones, just a rich sound all around. And they can get loud! Not always a requisite, but as Jerry Garcia said to Grisman during between-song banter on the famed *Pizza Tapes* sessions: 'On this planet, louder is better!' " ■

RADIO BRISTOL'S HIGH-TECH VINTAGE

Inside a hyper-local radio station blazing its own path into the future

by Thomas Grant Richardson

© BIRTHPLACE OF COUNTRY MUSIC

Radio Bristol producer Kris Truelsen

THE BIRTHPLACE OF Country Music Museum opened in the summer of 2014 in the border town of Bristol, where State Street is literally the state line between Tennessee and Virginia. Memorialized by Steve Earle in his bluegrass song "Carrie Brown," Bristol allows for an outlaw shootout to result in the lyric, "I shot him in Virginia and he died in Tennessee." More famously, Bristol is the site where RCA Records talent scout Ralph Peer recorded Jimmie Rodgers, The Carter Family, and a host of others in what would eventually become known as The Bristol Sessions. Hoping to capitalize on early success in the emergent market for "hillbilly" recordings, Peer sought a location where musicians could come to him instead of him tracking them down throughout the Appalachian region.

In the 1920s, hillbilly records had made early impressions — like when Peer recorded a few tracks of Fiddlin' John Carson in Atlanta, selling the 78s back to the local audiences — but until that summer in 1927, there hadn't been any major recording ventures into the southern Appalachian Mountains. But the artists recorded during those foundational weeks in Bristol went on to become household names, thereby kickstarting an industry that migrated from Bristol to Johnson City and Knoxville, Tennessee, years before settling into Nashville.

Nearly everything that followed in the country music industry would point back to the success and influence of those early Bristol recordings, leading country music scholar Nolan Porterfield to declare them the "Big Bang of Country Music." The Birthplace of Country Music Museum seeks not only to inform visitors about these legendary recording sessions from 1927, but also to showcase the effect they've had, and continue to have, on country music through the past century.

Radio as Exhibit

Visitors to the museum are guided through the story of The Bristol Sessions and how that "big bang" has affected the development of country music in general. About midway through the permanent exhibit sits Radio Bristol, WBCM, a station with one control room and a small studio for live on-air performances. Museum visitors can witness live radio being

MALCOLM WILSON

produced just beyond signage that contextualizes the role of radio in country music's dissemination and popularity. A dial connected to a pair of headphones allows visitors to hear historical recordings of WSM (Grand Ole Opry, from Nashville), WLS (*National Barn Dance*, Chicago), XET (border radio featuring The Carter Family), and WCYB (*Farm and Fun Time*, Bristol).

The station was originally planned as a static display featuring mannequins portraying work at a mock station, but that design didn't sit well with the original curatorial and design team. Dr. Jessica Turner, former head curator and museum director, recalls the shift in plans as the exhibits were taking shape. "As scholars we knew radio was essential to the story. But there's nothing exciting about looking at mannequins," she says. "It's also expensive. So we had a total rethink of the design, and decided for the amount of money those figures would cost us, we could make many of the exhibits really interactive — including the radio station!"

Along with the decision to opt for live broadcasters rather than mannequins, the curatorial team needed to reconsider the hardware required for a radio station. The control room now needed to serve double duty — to showcase historic, museum-quality radio equipment and to function as a fully operational station. Moreover, the station had to allow for conventional radio broadcasts, but it also needed to handle new digital methods, including streaming online. The exhibit text traces the roots of this old-meets-new station, stating that "the Raytheon RC-10 console was originally used at WCYB Radio" and noting it needed some technical upgrades: "masterfully rebuilt [by TNN/CMT audio engineer Jim

Farm and Fun Time in the performance theater

Gilmore] with modern specifications while retaining its original aesthetic."

The large RCA 44 ribbon microphone that was originally used by local Bristol radio announcer Tennessee Ernie Ford at WOPI reinforces the retro look and local connections. Yet for all these vintage touches, the station broadcasts digitally and can be accessed via smartphone app.

This combination of original aesthetics and modern specs could be considered the guiding force behind Radio Bristol; it's a mix Turner refers to as "high-tech vintage."

Jim Gilmore's rebuilding skills are geek-out worthy. Combining vintage and modern parts for a fully functional modern station proved to be a huge challenge, but resulted, according to Gilmore, in a control room that is "fully functional as a tracking, recording, production, and on-the-air studio for use by museum staff in producing programming, disc restoration, and as a museum attraction to give visitors a glimpse of what a radio station control room looked like at a time in our lives when broadcasting was an important part of our culture."

Gilmore's devotion to a bygone era when broadcasting was king has been taken up as a challenge by Radio Bristol, whose programmers believe it can be again. Rather than railing against modern trends of musical distribution, diffusion, and reception, Radio Bristol has sought not only to harness the technical possibilities of radio via online distribution, but also to tap into the current vogue of vintage, old-time, heritage products that seek to ameliorate the homogenization of American culture.

Radio as Concept

At WBCM-LP, Radio Bristol, DJs sit behind a console in the control room, speak into a microphone, and play music. That music can come off CDs, digital files, and quite often from vinyl LPs, 45s, and 78s. The music is sent out into the air via radio waves (the transmitter is attached to antennae broadcasting WOPI, now a sports station) and can get picked up on any dial in the area tuned to 100.1 FM. These days, the radios are usually in people's cars. And when driving around Bristol itself, the signal is strong and clear, even though this part of Appalachia is broken up with hills and hollers. However, the signal doesn't last long outside of town. As the "LP" after the station's name indicates, the signal is "low power," and without the use of a translator, it extends to an approximate 15-mile radius from the station.

"You start to lose it around Piney Flats," says Dr. René Rodgers, the Birthplace of Country Music Museum's current head curator.

But the terrestrial presence anchors Radio Bristol in the legacy and format of classic radio, which is important to locals. Bristol has a significant history with terrestrial radio. In 1946 Bristol had two stations playing country music: WCYB-AM and WOPI-FM, the latter of which became the region's first FM radio station.

While Radio Bristol's current 15-mile range is significantly less than that of even the stations of the 1940s, it has extended its reach considerably with the help of modern technology. The station has launched a web player and smartphone app where listeners can access a live feed of the daily programming from WBCM, as well as two digital playlists — "Americana" and "Classic."

These playlists are in line with the message of the museum, which is to showcase the original 1927 Bristol

PHOTOS BY BILLIE WHEELER

The museum's instrument case

Sessions not as a musical singularity, but as the "big bang" that spawned countless performers. On the "Classic" stream, a listener is likely to encounter The Carter Family, Bob Wills, or The Osborne Brothers, while the "Americana" stream features contemporary artists like Steve Earle, Tim O'Brien, Susan Tedeschi, and Buddy Miller. This is a logical spectrum from the organization that runs both the museum and the annual Rhythm & Roots Reunion, a staple of contemporary Americana festivals.

Radio Bristol producer Kris Truelsen says that the playlists were meant to fill up broadcast time when DJs were unavailable or the museum was closed (and therefore DJs couldn't broadcast), but that the number of listeners tuning into the live programming via the app or web player has "totally eclipsed" the streaming playlists. Currently the weekly program consists of 15 unique shows broadcast live from the museum. This schedule is complemented by another six specialized shows created elsewhere and sent in digitally and four nationally syndicated shows.

He acknowledges that it's a balancing act. "We're becoming more of a community radio station, which is good, but I need to make sure that the interpretation is also appropriate for the mission of the museum."

Truelsen and his team have become the de facto outreach program for the museum — part PR and part education — which is fitting given that Truelsen is a professional musician who received his master's degree in Appalachian studies from East Tennessee State University.

His morning show, *On the Sunny Side*, is a daily guided tour through the more particular (and often peculiar) annals of roots music history. Between tracks like Harry Belafonte's classic "The Banana Boat Song (Day O)," Bo Carter's double entendre song, "Banana in Your Fruit Basket," and the Hoosier Hotshots' "I Like Bananas Because They've Got No Bones," listeners get bits of information like how the 1876 Philadelphia Centennial Exposition introduced bananas to North America. This is not programming you'd find on any of iHeartMedia's nearly 900 radio stations. The live programming echoes an era of radio nearly extinct today.

Since the Telecommunications Act of 1996, which deregulated how many radio stations could be owned by a single corporation, independent radio has been slowly disappearing, as consolidation into fewer corporate owners has brought greater homogenization of the music played on air. Radio Bristol is bucking that trend with shows like *Diggin' With Big Lon.* Hosted by rare record collector Lonnie Salyer, the show is entirely dedicated to playing cuts from small, regional labels (many of which are defunct) recorded by musicians from central Appalachia. Such efforts would be laughable to large media companies. This means that it's up to community radio to highlight local tastemakers, music historians, and marginalized genres.

In addition to providing that hyper-local service, Radio Bristol's programming also echoes the theme of the museum, showcasing historical country music and connecting the dots through various subgenres like old-time mountain music, bluegrass, honky-tonk, contemporary Americana, and even occasionally rock and roll, soul, and pop music that's had an effect on country music. Rodgers, the head curator, says that programming is very intentional. "We can't have just anything on the air," she says. "It's about thinking deeply about how it fits in with the greater intention of the organization itself, how it reflects the mission and the story of the museum."

Of course, competing for attention on the internet is even harder than fighting for a piece of the corporate media pie. In order to drive traffic, attention, and awareness to the programming of Radio Bristol, it needed something big and attention grabbing. According to Truelsen, "When people hear Radio Bristol they know they're going to hear music from this region. The way to make it big is to make it small."

Radio as Community

The cornerstone of Radio Bristol's connection to the past is the revival of the flagship live show *Farm and Fun Time*. Originally a daily noontime show on Bristol's WCYB in the 1940s and 1950s, the program showcased bluegrass and country music. (WCYB stopped transmitting as a radio station in 1969 and today the call letters are assigned to a local NBC television affiliate.) The original *Farm and Fun Time* featured then up-and-coming acts like Mac Wiseman, Jimmy Martin, Flatt and Scruggs, Jim and Jesse, and The Stanley Brothers.

The new *Farm and Fun Time* was officially rebooted the day the museum opened in August 2014. The inaugural live performance featured Ralph Stanley and Jesse McReynolds, the latter playing the fiddle that his grandfather, Charlie McReynolds, used on a Bristol Sessions recording as a member of The Bull Mountain Moonshiners. The debut episode was hosted by local TV personality Johnny Wood and featured Truelsen's Blue Ridge Entertainers as the house band.

However, it took nearly a year before the reboot of *Farm and Fun Time* became a regular program. In that time, Truelsen went to work retooling, rethinking, and refining the show. According to former museum director Turner, "Kris studied that pilot and figured out what [the show] would need to be tight, informative, and entertaining. And Kris is a perfectionist, so it took a little time."

Truelsen took over as producer of the

NEIL STAPLES

monthly live broadcast, working closely with engineer and technical administrator Josh Littleton to create a throwback radio show that spoke simultaneously to historical and contemporary music and regional culture. Performed live each month in the museum's 100-seat theater, *Farm and Farm Time* features two visiting musical acts, an heirloom recipe from locals (such as pimento cheese, cornbread, or chess pie), and the Radio Bristol Farm Report, all pulled together by Truelsen's other band, Bill and The Belles.

In addition to serving as musical hosts, Bill and The Belles also continue the tradition of custom jingles for sponsors. Written by the band, these jingles — in the vein of Flatt and

Scruggs' "Martha White Theme" that touted the magic of self-rising flour — musically celebrate local businesses such as Eastman Credit Union. Tickets for *Farm and Fun Time* have consistently sold out for the past two years, and the show reaches ever farther via the radio and a broadcast of live video via the station's Facebook page.

"It's crazy to see who watches," says Truelsen. "We can track who's tuning in and where they're from. People all over the world are watching on Facebook."

As Radio Bristol grows and develops, it is still searching for new ways to impact the local community and influence the larger roots music world. The station is incorporated into the Birthplace of Country Music Museum's summer music camps and youth programs that partner with local organizations. And it showcases live broadcasts from local and touring musicians on an ongoing basis through its Radio Bristol Sessions. It has also gone mobile as an on-site broadcaster from events like the International Bluegrass Music Association's annual conference.

Even after just a few years, the effects of the museum and the station are being felt both locally and farther afield. Truelsen says many of the downtown shops and restaurants play Radio Bristol, enabling the station to be part of the soundscape of the town. Additionally, local breweries and coffee shops have begun showcasing live country and Americana music on a regular basis. Some in Bristol — like The Earnest Tube recording studio, which cuts directly to lacquer like Ralph Peer did in 1927 —have taken even bigger steps toward advancing this "high-tech vintage" sound.

Just as the town of Bristol itself straddles the line between two states, Radio Bristol — along with The Birthplace of Country Music Museum and local businesses that have tapped into the energy of the region's music — has found a way to keep one foot firmly planted in the past even as the other is staking a claim to the future. ■

Tim Easton

Old School Ways

by Tim Easton

THE FIRST TIME I SAW THE word "traditional" after a song title was on an album my sister had called The *History of the Grateful Dead.* The tune was a cinematic murder ballad named "I've Been All Around This World." The lyrics spoke of mountains, family, love, guns, murder, and capital punishment. Over the next three decades of traveling with my trusty black Gibson J-45, including seven years spent as a street musician in Europe, I worked that story song into my own style by tuning the guitar to open C, altering the rhythm, and adding a Delta-inspired slide part. All I had to do was write my own lyrics and it would become my own song.

In the hills near where I live in Whites Creek, Tennessee, I did just that. Geographically, I kept the location up high above sea level, and I also kept the standard country blues two-line couplet with a third answering line, took out the gunplay and murder, and made it my own tune called "Broken Hearted Man." The central characters are identical, except that in my tune there would be acceptance involved. Rather than end in tragedy, a truce is called and the protagonist survives.

I've taught a few songwriting workshops in Alaska, which is really just a good excuse to go fishing and camping and eat good food with friends up north. The first exercise is always to take an old folk or traditional song, change the melody, perhaps the meter, and write your own story to it. I learned this early on from Woody Guthrie, who did this very thing hundreds of times and often wouldn't even bother changing the melody.

When it came time to make my most recent record, *Paco & The Melodic Polaroids,* I wanted the recordings to be immediate and performance-based. I chose to record these 10 songs directly to lacquer in Bristol, Virginia, at a studio called The Earnest Tube, run by two friends from Cleveland, Ohio.

In this truly old-school form of recording, you record the song in mono (through one microphone) directly to a lathe, which cuts the signal into a spinning lacquer disc. There is no room for second-guessing your performance. When you are done singing and playing the song, no further manipulation is possible. This is how Ralph Peer recorded The Carter Family and Jimmie Rodgers for The Bristol Sessions, and how Alan Lomax captured all those field recordings we know today to be the foundation of our American music.

Paco & The Melodic Polaroids is a bit of a rambling, traveling love letter to my beloved Gibson guitar, named Paco in 1990 by a Deadhead in Paris. Aside from a difficult-to-find direct-to-cassette EP that Paco and I recorded in Prague around 1992, this is the only album I've made where I am the only musician performing and Paco is the only guitar used. I think of both of these projects as timestamps, sincere folk albums in that they capture very specific periods in my life and use no artifice in the process. I have found that these types of recordings retain the humanity that has been erased from many of our contemporary albums.

The Earnest Tube, run by Clint Holley and Dave Polster, started as a direct-to-lacquer studio in tribute to the legendary Bristol Sessions that took place right around the corner. However, it's also a multi-track facility, and Holley and Polster also run Well Made Music, a full-service mastering studio in Cleveland that has cut the vinyl masters for many

MICHAEL WEINTROB

recent albums.

During *Paco & The Melodic Polaroids*' release week earlier this year, I traveled to Cleveland to visit Well Made Music, see the mastering studio and lathe, and perform the album in its entirety in an art gallery located in the same building.

A lot of my touring and promotion of this album has focused on community building and has included a number of house shows and pop-up performances. It's been nice to apply the folk process to the touring life as well as the recording process, and to work with other creative types who are beginning to flourish in the ever-changing music business.

I also got to speak with Holley about the nuts and bolts of direct-to-lacquer recording.

TIM EASTON: What exactly is direct-to-lacquer recording? Explain the nitty-gritty.

CLINT HOLLEY: Recording to disc is a process that is now about 100 years old. The general idea is to take a blank disc (lacquer or wax) and "carve" the audio vibrations onto the soft surface using a sharp stylus that is vibrated by a transducer or cutter head. The transducer in effect is a "reverse microphone" that changes the electrical signal from a microphone back into the vibrations that make up music. Before electrical microphones, the performer shouted as loud as possible into a horn that funneled the acoustic energy directly to the cutter. ... These master recordings could then be turned into stampers that were used to make 78 rpm records before the advent of the 33 1/3 and 45 rpm formats.

TE: Where did you find your lathe and why did you want to buy one in the first place?

CH: I grew up collecting records when they went out of fashion in the 1980s. My parents took me to a lot of flea markets and LPs were selling for a dime or quarter each, and as a young person with limited financial resources, I could hear a lot of music on a small budget. Since that time, I have been fascinated by records. When a pressing plant opened in Cleveland in 2009, I saw a chance to make a career move. I had been a live sound engineer at a local rock club for nine years and I was burned out. The pressing plant did not hire me, but the owner took me on a day trip to see a cutting lathe in action as a consultant because I had a lot of audio experience. The person we visited did not have time to cut all the records that were in demand so my wife convinced me that I should find a lathe of my own. I did. A fellow named Albert Grundy, who was 82 when I met him and now deceased, became my mentor and sold me a Neumann VMS70 mastering lathe. That is how Well Made Music started.

In the end, though, I love being in the studio at the moment of creation, so my partner and I decided our skills as disc-cutting engineers could be put to good use in the studio. We traveled to a spot near Ocean City, Maryland, to buy a

Clint Holley records Tim Easton direct-to-lacquer.

microphone from a guy and he said he had an old cutting machine in his bedroom. We took a look at it, and it was an old REK-O-KUT suitcase cutter. We bought that and assembled our first portable cutting rig, and that became the basis for The Earnest Tube. In the last two years, we have cut about 40 sessions.

TE: Why did you open The Earnest Tube?

CH: I am a country music nerd, plain and simple. I have always lived my life rooting for the underdog, and for me, traditional country music (and now what is called alt-country or Americana) is the music of the underdog. Broken hearts, broken dreams, and broken lives are scattered through the songs and history of country music. The Earnest Tube is located in Bristol, right on the Tennessee and Virginia border. That town is called "The Birthplace of Country Music" because in July of 1927 Ralph Peer from Victor Records recorded both Jimmie Rodgers and The Carter Family direct to disc and took the idea of recording and publishing rural music (which had been around for about five years) and helped, for better or worse, create the modern music industry as we know it. So for me, Bristol has a story to tell, and I want to be a part of that story. By working in the medium of lacquer disc recording we help connect artists to that history. I had been trying to get away from the Northern winters for a long time, and the idea of heading south had a lot of appeal to me. The music is still deeply rooted in the culture and people in the South. The idea here is to interact with music rather than just standing around trying to look cool in a studio. I have always wanted to be a part of that and now me and Dave [Polster] feel that this is the way to go about it.

TE: Why record direct to lacquer? What are the benefits and the downsides? What is easy, what is complicated?

CH: From an aesthetic point of view, sometimes less is more. Less gear, fewer tracks, less bullshit that gets in the way of a great song or performance. We don't think this is the solution to everybody's recording needs ... it is a choice. The artist chooses to lay their song/performance out there, warts and all, for the world to hear. That takes confidence and practice and a bit of chutzpah to pull it off. A jugband recorded with multi-track recording in a pristine room is *not* what a jugband really sounds like, so this process is a lot like a stompbox or a plug-in for your DAW [digital audio workstation]. You can expect this process to affect your audio in a certain musical way, and it does. There is nothing easy about the process, but being prepared as an artist and as an engineer helps out a lot. Downsides, I don't know: not being able to "fix it in the mix"? I am always looking for lightning in a bottle, and to me, this process helps the artist get to that moment. ■

PHOTOS COURTESY OF THE EARNEST TUBE

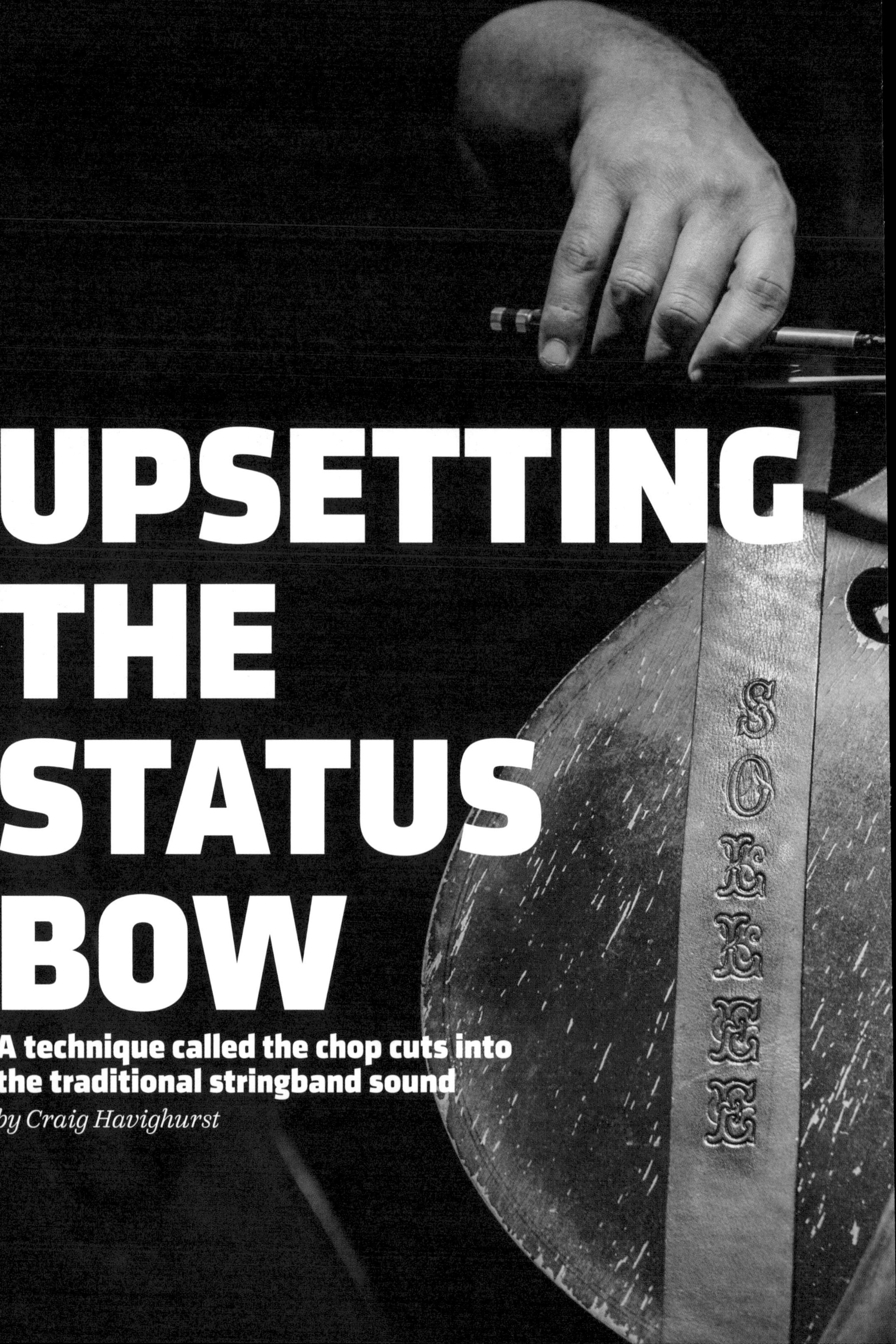

UPSETTING THE STATUS BOW

A technique called the chop cuts into the traditional stringband sound

by Craig Havighurst

MALLORY CUNNINGHAM

SPARE A THOUGHT FOR THE bow. Compared to the instruments whose strings they glide upon, the bow itself is more like an afterthought to most listeners. Yet, fiddle and bow make up a necessary, symbiotic relationship that goes back a thousand years.

According to one leading theory of unknowable events, Central Asian societies had three things in abundance — horses and horse hair, bows for shooting arrows, and rosin to improve one's grip. Some inventive musicians of the age figured out that horsehair stretched on a bow and rubbed with rosin could make stringed instruments emit sustained, singing notes. Humans had been plucking for centuries, so that realization must have been a novelty. A new musical mode, thus born, spread to China, Africa, and Europe.

By the 16th century the modern violin was developed, and in the late 18th century a Frenchman named François Xavier Tourte developed the archetypal Western bow. This bow, with its inward curve and adjustable tension nut, led to changes in the way musicians played the violin. So did the chin rest, which freed up the left hand to fly up and down the neck without having to do the work of holding the fiddle horizontal. But in a very general way, the basic business of animating stringed instruments with a bow remained the same for hundreds of years.

Then, in the late 20th century, this status quo was interrupted by a new technique. It proliferated through a generation of string players raised around fiddle camps, hip-hop, and globalism. This intricate method of turning a fiddle into crisp, funky percussion instrument with bow strikes and scrapes came to be called the chop. Fiddlers who'd spent hours of their youth learning proper techniques to keep their bows from scraping or scratching were suddenly infatuated with the aesthetic and technical antithesis — using the bite of a bow against the string as if it were a snare drum, a hi-hat, or a DJ scratching an LP.

"It was kind of earth-shattering," says Brittany Haas, who helped bring fiddle-based polyrhythmic soul to the

Laura Cortese

NATALIE CHAMPA JENNINGS

innovative Boston band Crooked Still, as well as more recently to the instrumental quartet Hawktail and the Dave Rawlings Machine. "It's really taken over, because once you have it you want to use it. There's so much you can do, thinking like a drummer."

Transgressive, transformative, and irresistible, chopping has disrupted traditional music, but also has helped it immeasurably by becoming a hook for younger musicians. It's a way to dial up the edge and funk of old-time, bluegrass, Celtic, and Canadian fiddling. Fiddle camps, where the chop went viral, were largely gray-haired affairs in the 1980s. The chop invited in a youth brigade and gave them something all their own.

A Recent History

Musical techniques usually emerge without clear provenance. Chopping, however, has been traced back to its headwaters, because its founders are all living and working. Montreal-based scholar and fiddler Laura Risk published the definitive history of the chop in a paper for the Society of Ethnomusicology called "The Diffusion of an Instrumental Technique across North Atlantic Fiddling Traditions," and it starts with the boundary stretching, Los Angeles-raised fiddler Richard Greene.

When Greene joined Bill Monroe and the Blue Grass Boys in 1966, Risk explains, Monroe told him he had a problem with rushing and commanded him to play no fills or figures when he wasn't soloing, only to tap out the beat with the tip of his bow. This proved fatiguing, so he shifted his tap to the frog of the bow, where the horsehair is especially taut. He found when he dropped the bow on the string and let it rest, it made a pronounced bark that served the rhythm of driving bluegrass. He also realized that besides the atonal chop of the downstroke, pulling the bow off the strings with a bit of friction could result in a sound that was pitched, yet percussive. He played with the ideas in a rock band called Sea Train, but a fuller realization of the musical possibilities of the chop had to wait until he taught it to another fiddler, Darol Anger, in the mid-1970s.

Anger was and remains one of the most eclectic and forward-thinking musicians who's ever played the fiddle/violin. He first began applying his newfound chopping technique with the David Grisman Quintet, a perfect vehicle for groove with its jazz, gypsy, and Latin influences. But Anger has written that the chop truly came into its own when he formed the Turtle Island String Quartet (TISQ) in 1984. Started as a jazz ensemble with a classical form, the TISQ was sophisticated, accessible, and deeply rhythmic, and all four instruments chopped in careful synchronicity.

"The chop made it possible for an acoustic string quartet to convincingly communicate the feeling of an entire jazz or contemporary pop group, without having to limit itself to just a 'chords, lines, and solos' section," Anger writes. "The TISQ was the first string quartet to really deliver the feeling of a full contemporary band with drums, guitar, bass, and improvising soloists, with a real live world-class groove."

This sojourn in contemporary art music was pivotal for the chop. The technique was put through rigorous paces in a relatively formal environment before it cycled back to folk and vernacular forms. That happened when Anger began teaching his refined and practiced version of the chop to young people at fiddle camps. Few picked it up with as much fervor or focus as Chicago-based Casey Driessen.

Finding a Way to Fit

Even when he was a kid in a youth bluegrass band, Driessen was trying to play rhythm with his bow. His band lacked a mandolin player, and he intuited ways to make his fiddle play the offbeats. Eventually people began telling him to check out Darol Anger, and around the time he enrolled in the Berklee College of Music, Driessen got personal instruction in the chop from the pioneer himself and began making a methodical study on his own as well.

"I spent a lot of time isolating all those movements and practicing them to be able to add them all together within a more complex rhythm, much like drummers do with independence between their right and left hand and their feet," Driessen says. "At Berklee I was around drummers and bass players, so I had to rethink my rhythm and how it could be applied to chopping. I was hanging out with people who were playing funk, R&B, hip-hop, soul, and pop, and I was trying to find ways to fit into these groups."

But he also developed and refined ways to make chopping a solo endeavor. His fiddle/vocal arrangement of "Working on a Building" is a tour de force of funky syncopation. He perfected new techniques, including an uncanny triplet figure made by skating the bow across the strings very fast but under control. Driessen himself became a major node of transmission, teaching it to a number of his peers, including Laura Cortese.

The leader of the stringband Laura Cortese and The Dance Cards grew up attending fiddle camps in California and then college at Berklee as the chop proliferated among younger players. She remembers being at the Celtic Connections festival in Glasgow when Driessen, already a friend, showed her his latest breakthrough, chopping and singing at the same time an arrangement of Paul McCartney's "Blackbird." "You have to figure out how to do this!" he urged.

She did, and the results were far deeper than merely adding a new trick to her act. "I was touring around playing

"It's really taken over, because once you have it you want to use it. There's so much you can do, thinking like a drummer."

Brittany Haas

my music with a band, and it always felt like the fiddle was an accessory," she said. "I just always felt like I wasn't getting to be at the core of the music. I was just sort of floating on top of whatever bed they laid down."

Forced by circumstances to downsize a trio into a duo, she finally integrated the chop at a level that changed everything. "I had to be the rhythm section and I had to be the chords. I had to be a major structural part of every song and be the lead singer. It was a great chance for me to figure out how to [put] the thing I grew up doing and that felt most authentic at the core of my music. And the chop really facilitated that."

Haas grew up attending some of the same fiddle camps as Cortese, and the chop helped her find new realms of musicality in a full band setting. She studied directly with Anger and toured with his boundary-pushing Republic of Strings. Then she joined one of the most rhythmic stringbands of all time, the Boston quartet Crooked Still. "Chopping ended up being a big thing propelling the groove in that band," Haas says. "We didn't have a guitar or a mandolin, [so] there's some rhythmic space that the bowed instruments are taking up."

In her current band Hawktail, she balances her rhythmic contributions with the more conventional chop of mandolinist Dominic Leslie. It's been a sequence of experiences designed to force thinking about where and when and how much chopping is appropriate.

The chopping cello, which seems to have started with the TISQ founding member Mark Summer, has become a thing in itself because of the instrument's rich tonality and physical differences compared to the horizontal violin or viola. Rushad Eggleston, who preceded Tristan Clarridge in Crooked Still, emerged as an innovator and whimsical pied piper for the chopping cello. Another, working as a songwriter in a very different context, was Kentucky's Ben Sollee.

"[The cello] just has more mass, so it takes more energy to move the strings, but you also have a lot more of the weight of your arm behind it," says Sollee. "And of course, the strings being lower, the chop is less of a hi-hat element or a snare element and it's more tucked in. That does change some things in an ensemble."

Sollee spent years on his own as a kid trying to get fresh and weird sounds out of his cello. He deeply identified with TISQ's Summer but didn't get to be around people chopping until a fiddle camp in about 2004. It was a life-changing experience, he says.

"I saw it and immediately said, 'You gotta show me.' " And he remembers Natalie Haas, Brittany's sister, doing just that. Soon after, Sollee wound up with Driessen in The Sparrow Quartet, where they played off one another and the banjos of Béla Fleck and Abigail Washburn. Sollee credits sitting next to Driessen for several years with refining his control of timbre and economy of motion.

But also he talks about growing up with a father who plays guitar in R&B bands, heavy doses of Motown, and a profound influence from the late hip-hop producer and rhythmologist J Dilla as the background for the way he integrates chopping into his music

Hawktail

JODY MARCH

today. "It's not just a percussive element to put in between some cool licks," he says. "I love playing beats on the cello and singing with them. For me, chopping is part of this palette of sounds I'm using to tell stories, as a songwriter. It's very important that those sounds and the gestures behind them back up the story."

Part of the Toolkit

Today, almost 50 years since Richard Greene taught the proto version to Darol Anger, chopping is a widely understood and widely taught tool, part of being a complete string player. Today the vital lessons in the technique are the taste and selectivity that needs to attend it. "Now it's been around long enough that it's taken on a life of its own," says Haas. "It's another texture to use where we see fit. It doesn't always need to be there."

To see where the chop is heading, watch over the shoulder of Driessen, who as director of the contemporary performance master's degree program for Berklee in Valencia, Spain, is working with Barcelona's Oriol Saña to develop a definitive notation system for the chop so that it can leap from the purview of improvisers into the kit bag of composers.

With its evocation of hatchets and axes, the chop is a peculiar term indeed for a technique applied to fine and often expensive wooden instruments. It conjures the same disobedient tone as the defining rhythmic breakthrough at the dawn of hip-hop. There are few things worse you can do to a vinyl record than scratch it, after all. The scratch and the chop are musicological cousins, paradoxes of progress. The chop sent ripples through roots music, destabilizing tradition in the most constructive way, inviting in new players and conjuring new cultural vocabulary. The chop is now everywhere, yet nobody and nothing has been cut off. ■

PLUGGED IN

The parallel journeys of three American masters who went electric and shook the world

by Matt Powell

ROZ LEVIN

Muddy Waters

“At night in the country, you’d be surprised how that music carries. The sound be empty out there. You could hear my guitar way before you get to the house, and you could hear the peoples hollerin’ and screamin’.”

Muddy Waters

ERNEST TUBB AND MUDDY Waters represent two sides of the same musical coin. They entered and left this world a year apart from each another. They both grew up in poverty, picking cotton as sharecroppers in Texas and Mississippi, respectively. They saw their music as a means to a better life, and they each developed their sound initially by copying established musical elders with whom they had some form of direct contact (Jimmie Rodgers for Tubb, Son House for Waters). Even their surnames evoke a certain symbiosis.

The arc of their careers align in key ways as well. While both Waters and Tubb began playing acoustic music (Delta blues for Waters and “hillbilly” for Tubb), it wasn’t until they discovered the power of the electric guitar that their music took on universal impact. With electric guitars, Waters and Tubb reinvented their respective genres, creating entirely new aesthetic standards and aural vocabularies, which in turn profoundly influenced newer genres of music, specifically rock and roll. They were visionaries, yet they plugged in out of necessity. They were revolutionaries, even as they remained traditionalists, growing gracefully into elder statesmen and musical ambassadors.

When Bob Dylan plugged in a generation later, he had the advantage of developing his music within the context of the electrified country and blues Tubb and Waters had already forged. But Dylan had established himself as an acoustic folk singer-songwriter in the early 1960s, copying the style of Woody Guthrie. When he went electric it was as revolutionary a choice as it was for Tubb or Waters in their time. Motivated by an artistic necessity to reinvent himself, Dylan rejected the confines of the folk music tradition while embracing the sonics of Waters’ and Tubb’s amplified innovations.

All three were met with resistance and calls of apostasy. But by remaining true to their vision as they each responded to an ever-loudening world, they forever changed the landscape of American music.

Crisp, Clarksdale, and Hibbing

Ernest Tubb was born on a cotton farm in Crisp, Texas, in 1914, the son of sharecroppers — a rambling, gambling alcoholic father, and a half-Cherokee orphaned mother. He grew up picking cotton alongside African Americans, where he learned to sing the blues. School was a four-mile walk into town, so he quit after 17 months. He later taught himself math and crammed his tour bus quarters with stacks of paperbacks.

His mother's credo, recalled in Ronnie Pugh's *Ernest Tubb: The Texas Troubador*, had a lasting impact on young Ernest: "Treat other people right, and you'll come out well in the end," she would say. As a country music superstar, Tubb closed his shows with a variation of that rule: "Be better to your neighbors, and you're gonna have better neighbors, doggone ya."

After his parents divorced, Tubb and his mother shared a wooden shack on the cotton farm. His older sister came to visit one day singing a Jimmie Rodgers song. Suddenly everything made sense.

Rodgers was a kind of modernist hillbilly superstar and an itinerant bluesman. Tubb was transfixed, even though he had yet to hear an actual Jimmie Rodgers recording. In a 1977 interview with the Grand Ole Opry's Hairl Hensley, Tubb recalled his sister teaching him the song and trying to explain Rodgers' trademark "blue yodel:" "He does a little hollering or something in there." Working at his father's filling station the following summer, Tubb discovered his dad's Jimmie Rodgers 78s. Without a guitar, Tubb went off into the fields to practice yodeling like his new hero.

Tubb wandered Texas, working odd jobs and singing on local radio. He slept in ditches and worked the fields, singing Jimmie Rodgers songs at house parties. Hitchhiking to San Antonio after a stint paving highways, he stopped in Abilene, where he bought a guitar for $5.50 at a pawn shop, and then walked the rest of the way.

When his musical hero died of tuberculosis in 1933, Tubb set to teaching himself guitar each night and perfecting Rodgers' "blue yodel." Then he opened the phone book, looked up Rodgers' widow, and dialed the number.

One year after Tubb was born, 450 miles away, McKinley Morganfield was born on the Stovall Plantation, outside of Clarksdale, Mississippi. "Muddy," as he was called, began to find music by banging on an old kerosene can, then a busted accordion, Jew's harp, and harmonica, before making his first

Bob Dylan

guitar out of a box and a stick.

Waters supplemented his sharecropping selling moonshine. Never afraid to embrace technology, he used the extra change to buy a 1934 V8 Ford. He was also entranced by his neighbor's phonograph. "She used to let us go over there all the time, and I played it night and day," he told Robert Palmer in the book *Deep Blues*.

He sold a horse, bought a used Stella guitar, and started gigging for $2.50 a night. He soon ordered an $11 Sears Roebuck Silvertone acoustic, playing with a slide the way Son House had taught him, and he'd seen Charley Patton and Robert Johnson in person.

The slide transformed acoustic guitars from mere rhythm accompaniment to a lead instrument. And it made it louder. (House, and Waters, sometimes used an aluminum-cone resonator guitar for added volume.) With the slide, Waters' guitar could cut through the lonesome Delta nights or keep the attention of rowdy juke joint patrons. "At night in the country, you'd be surprised how that music carries. The sound be empty out there," Waters said in *Deep Blues*, "You could hear my guitar way before you get to the house, and you could hear the peoples hollerin' and screamin'."

Legendary archivist and field recorder Alan Lomax recorded Waters on the plantation in 1941 with his portable tape recorder for the Library of Congress. Waters was inspired when he heard himself played back for the first time. The $20 Lomax sent him for the session also got his attention.

Technological advances in recording were making stars of blues singers. And machines were threatening sharecroppers' livelihoods, such as they were. Waters already had family in Chicago who had written home describing the opportunity there *making* those machines. After an argument with the new plantation manager in 1943, Waters took the session money and his Silvertone and caught the next train on the Illinois Central railway to Chicago.

A few months before Muddy Waters made his field recordings for Alan Lomax on the plantation, Bobby Zimmerman was born in the mining town of Hibbing, Minnesota. Unlike Tubb and Waters, Bobby was not a sharecropper; he grew up in postwar middle class comfort and boredom. He listened to Hank Williams, but pounded out Little Richard rock and

PHOTO BY DIANA DAVIES, COURTESY OF THE RALPH RINZLER FOLKLIFE ARCHIVES AND COLLECTIONS, SMITHSONIAN INSTITUTION

roll with his band on high school auditorium pianos. As the story is told in Martin Scorsese's documentary *No Direction Home: Bob Dylan*, at one show, the school's principal even drew the curtain early on one of his rowdier performances.

Late at night in his room, he absorbed strange sounds from Shreveport, Louisiana, over radio station KTHS — John Lee Hooker, Jimmy Reed, Howlin' Wolf, and Muddy Waters.

He was into individualist rebels like Marlon Brando, James Dean, and Jack Kerouac. From the front row at a show in Duluth, along the same Highway 61 that traveled all the way down through Clarksdale, Mississippi, Bobby saw Link Wray, Ritchie Valens, and Buddy Holly — playing his sunburst Fender Stratocaster — three days before Holly and Valens perished in the Iowa snow.

Dylan was born electric. Then he heard an Odetta album. "Right then and there, I went out and traded my electric guitar and amplifier for an acoustical guitar, a flat-top Gibson," he said in a 1978 *Playboy* interview. After reading Woody Guthrie's *Bound for Glory*, his restless farewell was on.

Dylan heard that Guthrie lay dying in a New Jersey hospital. With the same impulse that brought Ernest Tubb to call on Jimmie Rodgers' widow, Dylan hitched a ride to the East Coast.

Make 'Em Louder

Tubb and Waters embraced the electric guitar for the same basic reason — to be heard in noisy barrooms. Their transition to electric happened around the same time, spawned by similar circumstances and motivations. Their journeys began with leaps of faith, with Waters' impulsive move to Chicago and Tubb cold-calling Jimmie Rodgers' widow.

Carrie Rodgers, moved by Tubb's sincerity, invited the aspiring singer for a visit. She let him hold her late husband's acoustic Martin D-45, with "Jimmie Rodgers" etched along the fretboard, later gifting the guitar to Tubb. More importantly, she arranged a recording session with RCA's Bluebird imprint, and two custom songs by her sister Elsie McWilliams, who had penned some of Jimmie Rodgers' songs. These records sold poorly — Tubb was still a mere Jimmie Rodgers clone — but he was now a recording artist.

Carrie Rodgers told him the best way to repay her was to help others. Reaching the heights of superstardom, Tubb dedicated as much of his efforts to helping the careers of others as his own: Loretta Lynn, Johnny Cash, Hank Williams, Hank Thompson, Hank Snow, Jack Greene, Cal Smith, Billy Walker, Stonewall Jackson, the Wilburn Brothers, and Elvis Presley all acknowledged debts to Ernest Tubb.

A tonsillectomy and a chance encounter forever changed the trajectory of his life. The doctor assured Tubb the procedure would not affect his singing voice. The reality was Tubb never yodeled again. He was devastated. Without the yodel, he wondered whether to sing Rodgers songs at all.

Tubb returned to the woodshed, developing, by necessity, his own unique singing style and writing his own songs: "Blue Eyed Elaine," "I'll Get Along Somehow," and "Try Me One More Time" are among the earliest.

He recorded a few sides for Decca, who offered Depression-era customers affordable "hillbilly" and "race" records. Tubb was building a reputation as a jukebox star — in the hillbilly market then, jukeboxes *were* the music business — but when he ran into a jukebox operator on the streets of Fort Worth one day, he learned there was a problem.

Tubb recalled to biographer Ronnie Pugh what the jukebox man told him: "In the afternoons, when just a few people are sitting around drinking beer in these joints where my boxes are, they'll play your records all afternoon. But as soon as the crowd gets in there and gets noisy, they start dancing, they can't hear your records, they start playing Bob Wills. They're not playing your records: you need to make them louder."

Tubb couldn't afford a big band like Wills and other western swing outfits. But Decca had another session booked, and Tubb knew he had written a hit. Electric guitars in 1941 were relatively uncharted territory. Gibson's hollow-body ES-150 was only a few years old, and expensive. Leo Fender was still a decade away from morphing the electric lap steel into his mass-produced, solid-body Telecaster. Tubb dropped $20 on a DeArmond electric pickup at a pawn shop and sent it to his guitar player, Jimmy Short, with the following note: "Learn to play electric: we gotta make 'em louder."

But Short couldn't get away from a gig in Nebraska, so Tubb found Fay "Smitty" Smith, a Fort Worth electric player who only comped chords and couldn't improvise.

Tubb told Smith to stick to the melody — a template that would define the Ernest Tubb sound for 40 years. At this session, Tubb strummed Jimmie Rodgers' Martin, exclaiming "ah, pick it out, Smitty," while Smith blared the electric lead on "Walking the Floor Over You." It was an instant smash, catapulting Tubb's career and birthing a new genre of hillbilly music — something different from western swing. Something that could keep you company on your stool in the afternoon and keep the dance floor hot long into the night. A blues for the working class — "impolite white society" — who were flocking to busier urban centers. Something that wasn't afraid to declare universal vulnerabilities openly: I'm *walking the floor* over you! Simple, honest, and loud, like the establishments for which it was custom tailored: honky-tonk.

Two years later, in 1943, Tubb moved to Nashville. That same year, Muddy Waters arrived in Chicago and, with overtime, made more money in one week in the factories than in a year picking cotton back in Mississippi.

The Chicago that Waters found in the early 1940s was still a jazz town. He played his acoustic Delta blues at house parties for other Deep South expatriates, but nobody wanted to hear what he called "sad old-time blues" around town. Nobody *could* hear it in the clubs among the roaring urban boom.

A friend of Waters' cousin named Jimmy Rogers started playing in the Delta on a one-stringed diddley bow, an instrument native to the rural South made by nailing a piece of wire to a slab of wood. Oftentimes, a glass bottle is used as the bridge. In Chicago, Rogers was amplifying his acoustic guitar with a DeArmond pickup. Waters followed suit, and they developed their electrified interplay together.

With Little Walter — who was discovering how an amplifier could dramatically change the parameters of what a blues harmonica could sound like — the trio worked up their new sound in South and West Side clubs, where they reinvented the country blues for the modern age, creating the concept of a blues band. With pianist Otis Spann, the legendary lineup was formed. Veteran Chicago players would apprentice in Waters' band over the years, but at its core remained Waters' distinct brand of Delta blues transfused with electric power.

Waters recorded "Rollin' Stone" for Chess in 1950, accompanying himself alone with his DeArmond-enhanced Gretsch. Half in the Delta and half in the future, the biting electric slide of "Rollin' Stone" set a generation on fire, inspiring a band name, a magazine, and a song title a Minnesota kid would use to harness his own electricity 15 years later.

How Does It Feel

Legend has it that Dylan's shift to electric was not developed out of necessity, like Ernest Tubb's and Muddy Waters', but was immaculately conceived one summer evening — July 25, 1965 — at the Newport Folk Festival.

But Dylan had released half an album of amplified music (side A of *Bringing It All Back Home*) and a current radio single ("Like a Rolling Stone") when he took the Newport stage in 1965. He'd brought an energy to Greenwich Village from his arrival four years earlier. "I played all the folk songs with a rock 'n' roll attitude," he said in the *Biograph* liner notes. "This is what made me different and allowed me to cut through all the mess and be heard."

Dylan operated outside of the folk tradition, constantly developing his artistry, rendering his most recent records obsolete by time of their release. But songs like "Blowin' in the Wind" cemented Dylan as the "spokesman for a generation." It didn't matter that he'd moved on.

The Newport Folk Festival grew out of the Newport Jazz Festival, where Muddy Waters played his electric Chicago blues loud and gritty in 1960. The polite jazz audience in the wealthy New England seaside town dug it as Waters thrusted and gyrated his hips while explaining how he got his mojo workin'. The footage reveals a juxtaposition of young white kids in bathing suits enthralled by the South Side bluesmen in their shiny mohair, buttoned collars, and pocket squares playing music that rocked every bit as much as The Rolling Stones later would — four years before the British Invasion.

Chuck Berry duckwalked with his electric guitar at Newport Jazz in 1958. John Lee Hooker plugged in at Newport Folk in 1963. Johnny Cash brought Fenders to Newport Folk in 1964, as did The Staple Singers, featuring Pops Staples' prominent vibrato-drenched electric guitar. Prior to Dylan's controversial 1965 set, The Chambers Brothers rocked the house, with Sam Lay on drums, who would also accompany Dylan that same weekend. After the Chambers' set, Alan Lomax told the crowd: "I'm very proud tonight that we finally got onto the Newport Folk Festival our modern American folk music: rock and roll!"

Electric guitars were nothing new to Newport or Dylan.

But at that time folk music was more of an ideology than a genre. And Dylan hardly subscribed to a branded ideology, even as he used its faithful to further his music.

Dylan's folk contemporaries were mostly middle class kids living in the collegiate safety of Washington Square or Cambridge who knew nothing about picking cotton or paving hot Texas highways. They didn't worry about jukebox sales or cutting through the juke joint noise of South Side Chicago.

Dylan didn't know these things, of course, but he was growing frustrated with the pretense of the folk music scene and its limitations. And he knew there was a world of music forbidden to him by "self-ordained professors' tongues." He had a genuine affinity for folk music, but he never had any use for the movement's political and communal restrictions.

"Bobby was not really a political person," Dave Van Ronk said in *No Direction Home.* "We thought he was hopelessly politically naïve. But in retrospect, I think he may have been more sophisticated than we were."

Dragged to a banquet to accept an award from a leftist organization he wanted nothing to do with, Dylan addressed the room that night: "There's no black and white, left and right to me anymore. There's only up and down, and down is very close to the ground, and I'm trying to go up without thinking about anything trivial such as politics."

The afternoon before Dylan's infamous Newport set, The Paul Butterfield Blues Band headlined a blues workshop, where their tough Chicago blues was met with derision by some of the old guard who felt this loud sound wasn't really *folk* music. Alan Lomax and Dylan's manager Albert Grossman got into a fistfight — during the set — which also drowned out Mother Maybelle's nearby autoharp workshop.

While some puritanicals believed the blues should stay in the Delta, the electric blues — as birthed by Muddy Waters and passed on to musicians like the Butterfield band — became to others a natural extension, not a bastardization, of the original form. This was what the real folk on the South and West sides of Chicago were hearing.

The son of an Irish immigrant, Paul Butterfield learned to blow blues harp by hanging around clubs since before he was old enough to get in, watching from the door. He and white friends, like guitarist Mike Bloomfield, immersed themselves in the music of Chicago's South Side, and eventually, local legends like Muddy Waters started inviting them to sit in.

Seeing that Bloomfield and Al Kooper, who both had played on his recent "Like a Rolling Stone" session, were at Newport, Dylan got an idea. Like Tubb and Waters, he needed to cut through the din to make himself heard too.

Dylan took the stage in a black leather jacket, brandishing a sunburst Stratocaster, flanked by Bloomfield, drummer Sam Lay, bassist Jerome Arnold, and Kooper on organ. There was chaos and confusion as the under-rehearsed band started blazing, full volume, distorted, out of sync, trying to find the groove in the noise. Bloomfield shouts, "Let's go!"

Dylan steps up to the microphone: "I ain't gonna work on Maggie's farm no more!"

Bob Dylan was done toiling amid the straight rows of folk music.

Well I try my best to be just like I am
But everybody wants you to be just like them
They say 'sing while you slave,'
I just get bored.

By most accounts, it was a mess, but nobody said it was boring. Jerome Arnold never could figure out the changes — he was a blues player, and the new music Dylan was making, while based in the blues, was something different.

Perhaps to quell the crowd, perhaps to rub it in, Dylan returned to the stage, alone, with an acoustic guitar and sang "It's All Over Now, Baby Blue."

"It was electric," Dylan said in *No Direction Home,* "but that doesn't necessarily mean it's modernized, just because it's electric. Country music was electric too."

The World Gonna Know

Country music was indeed electric, as Dylan noted, but it wasn't always so. In the 1940s, the Grand Ole Opry was even more averse to electric guitars than Newport was in the 1960s.

"We got one a-them things on the Opry and we couldn't stop it from hollerin', and it just *bellered* out and we got rid of that thing right fast," Roy Acuff recalled in the documentary *Thanks, Troubadour, Thanks.*

But when Ernest Tubb showed up for his Opry debut in 1943 with his electric guitar player in tow, he was one of Decca's biggest stars — second only to Bing Crosby — with multiple jukebox hits and Hollywood films to his name. Sinatra comparisons weren't unusual. Tubb brought national star power to the Opry, not the reverse.

Not even Acuff could deny the Texas Troubadour's electricity.

Tubb's amplified honky-tonk shaped a generation. Hank Williams confessed Tubb's profound influence on his vocal style (and "walking the floor" imagery for "Your Cheatin' Heart"). Tubb built up his Texas Troubadours band with virtuoso instrumentalists who knew their mission was to serve the song, letting them cut loose on the occasional jazzy instrumental and always calling out credit on records.

Like Waters, Tubb's band became a proving ground for legendary pickers, including electric lead guitarists Billy Byrd and Leon Rhodes.

Without compromising his honest, simple music, Tubb revolutionized the industry. Instrumental in building Nashville into Music City, he brought in the first major record label, Decca, and convinced them and the entire industry to reject the pejorative "hillbilly" label, insisting they call it "country music." "You can call me a hillbilly," he would say, "if you got a smile on your face."

Responding to a hungry and neglected national (and international) country music audience, Tubb opened his eponymous record shop, and its groundbreaking mail order service, in 1947. Insisting on replacing at his expense all records damaged in transit, it lost money for years, saved only by the less brittle 45 and 33⅓ technologies. He hired African Americans in his shop at a time when they couldn't sit at downtown Nashville lunch counters.

He started the *Midnite Jamboree* radio show, where stars and hopefuls alike kept the music going after the Opry, broadcast live from his record shop over WSM. Tubb felt folks who couldn't afford an Opry ticket deserved a show too, and anybody with the desire deserved a chance to be heard.

While Ernest Tubb was overseeing his position as a patriarch of the country music world in the 1950s and 1960s, Muddy Waters was discovering new audiences beyond his South Side neighborhood.

When Waters went to England in 1958, he brought the Telecaster he would play for the rest of his life, nicknamed "The Hoss." Waters' UK shows were met with the same derision and befuddlement as Dylan's would be in 1965. Dylan's British folk fans felt betrayed — Judas! they screamed — for Waters, the British harbored false expectations. "They wanted Muddy to be a folk musician," British photographer Val Wilmer told Waters biographer Robert Gordon, "and electric guitar had not really been heard, not loud." Critics walked out. One headline blared: "Screaming Guitar and Howling Piano." It wasn't a compliment.

"I had my amplifier and Spann and I was going to do a Chicago thing," Waters told James Rooney in *Bossmen*. "I was definitely too loud for them then."

Some young Brits, however, were turned on. Eric Burdon and John Steel formed The Animals, the toughest of the British invasion bands, shortly after witnessing Waters' Newcastle show. When Waters returned in 1963, England was sprouting bands with names like The Manish Boys, The Mojos, and The Rolling Stones.

It wasn't just the British; a whole generation of forward-thinking musicians were inspired by Waters' electrified "sad old-time blues."

"The first guitarist I was aware of was Muddy Waters," Jimi Hendrix told *Rolling Stone* in 1968, "I heard one of his old records when I was a little boy and it scared me to death, because I heard all of those sounds."

Bringing It All Back Home

Muddy Waters was called "boy" until he was 30. When he plugged in, he declared, "I'm a Man!" And lest he wasn't clear, he spelled it out: "M - A - N."

"I had it in my mind even then to either play music or preach or do something that I would be known, that people would know me," he said in *Bossmen*.

To many, he was a god, capable of conjuring sound and fury. From this perspective, perhaps he was declaring his mortality as much as his pride: I am *but* a man. Subject to the blues: I sin, I hurt.

Ernest Tubb fought for respectability in a cutthroat business. You'd best be smiling if you called him "hillbilly." Well into his final years, he waited after every show until every autograph was signed, every photo snapped. Only then would he get back on his Green Hornet bus, on to the next town to do it again, his singular purpose to reach people. No metaphor, no irony; only blunt truths: "I'll Get Along Somehow," "It's Been So Long Darling," "Pass the Booze." When on a tear, there could be tortured mornings. On stage, a big, sincere grin. He sacrificed himself for his fans — putting their struggles on his shoulders.

Bob Dylan's fans became irrational, forcing his public withdrawal even as he continues his "Never Ending Tour," surfacing only occasionally. He was a prophet before he was Judas. "He wanted more than anything else to be a rock and roll singer," high school girlfriend Echo Helstrom recalled in *Positively Main Street*. He cast off the "spokesman" shackles only to be imprisoned deeper in rock stardom.

In the new millennium, Dylan reinvented himself again as a "cowboy band" leader, dressing like a Texas Troubadour, surrounding himself with a loud, fine-tuned outfit serving his songs. Dylan keeps his music amplified and alive in front of the people, where it belongs. Like Waters in his latter-day revival and Tubb on his Green Hornet bus, they're all spokesmen, troubadours, rollin' stones.

Amid the gathering noise of Texas honky-tonks, South Side juke joints, and Greenwich Village hootenannies, Ernest Tubb, Muddy Waters, and Bob Dylan strove to be heard. Measuring the distance between the lightning and the thunder — between the music they were making and the sounds they knew they could — they tied a key to a kite and stepped out into the storm. ■

PHOTO COURTESY OF COUNTRY MUSIC HALL OF FAME® AND MUSEUM

Ernest Tubb

TOUGH OUTER SHELL

Following the birth and rebirth of outlaw country

by Hilary Saunders

JOHN SHEARER/GETTY IMAGES

ILLUSTRATION BY JIM FRANKLIN, COURTESY OF THE COUNTRY MUSIC HALL OF FAME AND MUSEUM

"Outlaw country was coined that not so much because these guys were getting speeding tickets or busted for drugs or cutting the tag off their mattress or whatever, but [because] they were not bending to the will of a higher corporate power."
Elizabeth Cook

THE ARMADILLO IS ONE UGLY creature. It's got a rodent face and rounded claws for burrowing deep into the land. It's got a prickly underbelly like a porcupine and a leathery exterior that looks like Old World armor. It's the only mammal with a shell, which led the Spaniards to name it "armadillo," translating to "little armored thing." Even before that, the Aztecs described this weird creature as a "turtle-rabbit."

Still, the armadillo is a feisty, self-sufficient being that can withstand extraordinary obstacles. Up to 100 teeth can be found inside one animal's mouth to prey on bugs, eggs, plants, and small vertebrates. One of the 20 species of armadillos can even curl up into a ball to protect itself from predators.

Thanks to this duality of tiny size and tough resilience, the armadillo became the symbol of a movement, too. Outlaw country music — an innovative subgenre of country marked by styles that alternated between raucously heavy and sparsely heartbreaking, combined with a musician-led rebellion for creative control over their work — clattered onto the scene in the 1970s, diverting from the glitz of Nudie suits along Nashville's Broadway and the dulcet Telecaster tones streaming from Music Row.

Outlaw country music, at its outset, represented "the melding of hippie and redneck cultures," according to Peter Cooper, senior director, producer, and writer of the Country Music Hall of Fame and Museum and co-curator of its current special exhibit called *Outlaws & Armadillos: Country's Roaring '70s*.

And as Eddie Wilson, founder of Austin, Texas' Armadillo World Headquarters club, once said to Chet Flippo at *Rolling Stone:* "Armadillos and hippies are somewhat alike, 'cause they're

JOHN SHEARER/GETTY IMAGES

maligned and picked on. ... People think they're smelly and ugly and they keep their noses in the grass. They're paranoid. But they've got one characteristic that nobody can knock: They survive like a sonuvabitch."

'The Roaring '70s'

Taylor Swift is in Nashville for a gig the day that Cooper and co-curator Michael Gray can meet and offer a tour of the *Outlaws & Armadillos* exhibit. These Swifties, dressed flawlessly in black and white *Reputation* swag and shiny, sequined accessories, buzzed around the exhibit in sharp contrast to the dusty, dirty, and sometimes even taboo legacy pieces from Willie Nelson, Bobby Bare, Cowboy Jack Clement, Jessi Colter, Kris Kristofferson, Waylon Jennings, Townes Van Zandt, and others that are preserved behind glass. The irony is palpable, as Swift represents much of what these outlaws rebelled against in the first place.

Having opened in late May, *Outlaws & Armadillos* is one of many exhibits currently on display in the Country Music Hall of Fame and Museum, and it will stay open until February 2021. Presented in an open space on the second floor, the exhibit tells "a tale of two cities — Nashville and Austin," says Gray, the senior museum editor and exhibit co-curator. Everything here, he explains with a small sweep of the hand, "would lead to Americana."

The space dedicated to *Outlaws & Armadillos* is divided into multiple sections. Around the outside of the room, videos tucked away in quiet corner viewing spaces play never-before-seen footage from some of the most famous outlaw country musicians. Glass cases filled with memorabilia and treasures (ranging from Kristofferson's US Army utility shirt to a copper whiskey still used by Reverend Will D. Campbell and Tom T. Hall to Joe Ely's Ringling Brothers circus coveralls, in addition to a slew of instruments) line most of the rest of the walls, while pyramid-like pillars with information on each of their three sides lead visitors along a loosely guided path. The parallel stories of the rise of outlaw country in Nashville and Austin start at opposite sides of the exhibit and meet in the middle.

Many of the videos come from the exhibit's third co-curator, Eric Geadelmann. The Austin-based filmmaker is working on a documentary series titled *They Called Us Outlaws*, produced by Crowfly Pictures Entertainment and Filament Productions and presented by the Hall of Fame. Geadelmann has enough material for a six-part, 12-hour film and provided the Hall of Fame with exclusive interviews and live performance footage collected

JOHN SHEARER/GETTY IMAGES

…UE BREWER, COURTESY OF MICHAEL CASEY.
…E ALBRIGHT, JESSI COLTER, AND WILLIE NELSON
IMAGES FROM THE CHET FLIPPO COLLECTION. IN ORDER OF APPEARANCE:
COMMANDER CODY, WAYLON JENNINGS, THE WAYLORS, PAUL ENGLISH, TOMPALL GLASER, AND WILLIE NELSON

HEARTWORN HIGHWAYS
The best music and the best whiskey come from the same part of the country.
GUY CLARK
DAVID ALLAN COE
LARRY JON WILSON
RODNEY CROWELL
STEVE YOUNG
CHARLIE DANIELS BAND
COACH ROYAL
CIRCUS

during his research.

The timing of the exhibit is intentional. Gray explains that the Hall of Fame's reasoning for an exploration of this innovative sect of country music came with three aligning factors. In addition to Geadelmann's upcoming film, the Hall of Fame had found some outlaw-era gems in the collections of Texas singer-songwriter Kimmie Rhodes (whose late husband, Joe Gracey, was a DJ, record producer, and talent coordinator for *Austin City Limits*) and music journalist Chet Flippo. And the timing of the outlaw movement chronologically (and coincidentally) followed that of the museum's previous exhibit, *Dylan, Cash, and the Nashville Cats*. The idea is to contextualize outlaw country's place in the rich history of country music, and to illustrate its continued relevance in Americana today.

A Tale of Two Cities

Especially within the context of the *Outlaws & Armadillos* exhibit, it's pretty easy to distill the history of the outlaw movement to two centralized places — Nashville and Austin. During the 1960s, a cadre of musicians soon to be known as "outlaws" all moved to Nashville. When they got there, though, they found the music industry machine rife with formalities and insularity, and the music itself polished with a flawless, insincere sheen.

Before the outlaw movement, Gray says with a laugh while pointing out old photos in the exhibit, "Willie looked like an insurance agent!"

Nelson, for his part, described the experience like this in his 2016 memoir, *It's a Long Story: My Life*: "With all the music coming out of Nashville — all the great musicians and legendary producers — you'd think I'd be a natural fit. I never was."

It had become standard practice at Nashville's major labels and recording studios for executives to determine an album's producer, session musicians, aesthetic, and even which songs the artists would record. As Waylon Jennings is quoted as saying in LeRoy Ashby's 2006 book, *With Amusement for All: A History of American Popular Culture Since 1830*, "They wouldn't let you do anything. You had to dress a certain way: you had to do everything a certain way."

By the 1970s, artists like Nelson and Jennings grew out their hair and beards, opted for leather jackets instead of rhinestone suits, and started co-writing and self-producing to combat the industry's rigidity and assert creative freedom. Bobby Bare was the first musician of the outlaw era to demand control of his record-making process. He migrated from RCA Victor to Mercury Records, but wound up back at the former when label head Chet Atkins coaxed him back with the promise of self-producing. The result was 1973's *I Hate Goodbyes / Ride Me Down Easy*.

Tompall Glaser's studio off Music Row, dubbed Hillbilly Central (now the headquarters for Compass Records), became home to many of the outlaw artists. Musicians including Kristofferson, Billy Joe Shaver, Jennings, Shel Silverstein (before he started writing children's' books and poetry), John Hartford, and more recorded in its fabled studio. Hazel Smith, who is credited with coming up with the "outlaw" term, even worked the front desk in the early stages of her illustrious Music City career.

Other defining records of the region and era included Jennings' *Honky Tonk Heroes* and Bare's *Bobby Bare Sings Lullabys, Legends, and Lies* (which was a collection of songs written by Silverstein). But it was actually Texan singer, songwriter, and satirist Kinky Friedman who seemed to summarize the general feeling in Nashville at the time. As he sings in the title track of his 1973 album *Sold American:*

Faded jaded falling cowboy star
Pawnshops itching for your old guitar
Where you're going, God only knows
The sequins have fallen
from your clothes
Once you heard the
Opry crowd applaud
Now you're hanging out at
Fourth and Broad
On the rain wet sidewalk
remembering the time
When coffee with a friend
was still a dime.

It was a poetic, yet pessimistic response to the Nashville Sound, an encapsulation of the outlaw mentality.

JOHN SHEARER/GETTY IMAGES

Willie Nelson and Waylon Jennings at Willie Nelson's Fourth of July Picnic, 1978.

Outlaw songs like these were "as much influenced by Hank Williams as William Blake ... ," Cooper says. "[They were] more literary songs, away from what Tom T. Hall called 'lil' darlin' songs.'"

But while Nashville had the fancy recording studios and industry (rigid as it was), Austin seemed to be the place for performing this music. As a result, many musicians zipped between the two hubs. Nelson, for example, moved back to Texas in 1969 after his Tennessee home caught fire. In 1973, he launched his annual Fourth of July Picnic concert (which is still running, although its locations have moved across Texas over the years). And in 1975, he recorded one of his biggest hit records, *Red Headed Stranger*, in Texas as well.

The live scene in Austin radiated from a venue called the Armadillo World Headquarters, which opened in the summer of 1970. Shortly thereafter, it became a hub not just for music, but also for psychedelic art and counterculture. The club with the weird animal mascot offered a live and visual element to these new outlaw sounds.

Many musicians waxed poetic about that community, regardless of where they were in the world. As the story goes, Gary P. Nunn penned an ode to Austin in 1973 while staying with a friend in London. Jerry Jeff Walker then recorded that song, "London Homesick Blues (Home with the Armadillo)," and released it on his breakthrough album *¡Viva Terlingua!* later that year.

I want to go home with the armadillo
Good country music from
Amarillo and Abilene
The friendliest people
and the prettiest women
You've ever seen.

Additionally, Austin and the Armadillo fostered a growing community of visual artists who responded and related to the outlaw movement. Between the show posters and fliers, pop-up murals, and album artwork, underground art helped give a look to the outlaw sound.

In fact, it was one of the leading visual artists of the '70s, Jim Franklin, who deemed the armadillo a metaphor for Austin's burgeoning countercultural scene.

"Franklin's remarkable art and anti-establishment outlook caught on, and the armadillo became the likeliest varmint to use in the title of the scene's gathering spot, the Armadillo World Headquarters," Cooper explains. And when the Hall of Fame began planning for *Outlaws & Armadillos*, Franklin's new painting of Willie Nelson, Waylon Jennings, and an armadillo became the lead image for the exhibit.

The Beginning of the End

By 1976 the outlaw movement had hit the mainstream. That year, RCA Records released a compilation record called *Wanted! The Outlaws* with tracks from Jennings, Nelson, Colter, and Glaser. The cover is stylized like an old Western poster, with headshots of the four musicians — often bearded or hatted —

PHOTOS BY LEONARD KAMSLER, COURTESY OF THE COUNTRY MUSIC HALL OF FAME AND MUSEUM

Bobby Bare

Tompall Glaser

presented like wanted fugitives. That album was the first country record to go platinum.

"For some reason that record sold shitloads," Bare told the *Nashville Scene* earlier this year. "They got labeled outlaws, but they never did take it very seriously. It was a PR game. They weren't outlaws — they were just creative people who loved music and hanging out."

Once the Music Row executives started to brand the outlaw mentality and latch onto the genre's singers and songwriters, those creating the music started to move on to new ideas and new sounds. By 1978, Nelson worked with producer Booker T. Jones on a record of standards and show tunes called *Stardust*. And later that year, Jennings penned the song that eventually became the anthem for the end of the era. That song, "Don't You Think This Outlaw Bit's Done Got Out of Hand," off his 1978 album *I've Always Been Crazy*, is an upbeat, twangy number that paints Music Row executives as law enforcement and ironically perpetuates the metaphor that he and other independence-seeking musicians were outlaws. Additionally, as Jennings was embroiled in his own cocaine addiction, the song represented a push for breaking his own habits that helped color the outlaw movement. By 1981, the Armadillo in Austin had shuttered.

Although the rise and fall of the outlaws was essentially contained within the 1970s, the genre represented an ideal more than a sound. As Kris Kristofferson said in an interview with Geadelmann during the filming of *They Called Us Outlaws*, "I don't think that would've been the brand name we would've chosen. To be outlaws. I think we went our own way and spoke our own words because we believed in them. And believed in that's what we were set down on the planet to do. We weren't worried about commerciality. Because it didn't make any difference if we were on *[Your] Hit Parade* or whether we were making a lot of money. It was whether we were doing the good work ... writing soulful songs."

Modern Reinventions

Within the past few years, the outlaw ideal has made a strong resurgence. Outlaws were all about creative freedom, which was especially innovative in the '70s, but they also helped pave the way for modern country musicians seeking more control over their own careers in the 21st century.

These days, many credit the return of the outlaw ethos to artists like Jamey Johnson, Sturgill Simpson, and Chris Stapleton, but it's been stirring a long time. In 2014, for example, SiriusXM launched its Outlaw Country satellite radio station (Channel 60). And even as far back as 2008, Nashville-based country singer-songwriter Elizabeth Cook (who hosts a show on SiriusXM's Outlaw Country station called *Elizabeth Cook's Apron Strings*) released "Sometimes It Takes Balls to Be a Woman" — a rebellion song still banned at the Grand Ole Opry, she notes with a laugh — on her album *Balls*.

Says Cook, "Outlaw country was coined that not so much because these guys were getting speeding tickets or busted for drugs or cutting the tag off their mattress or whatever, but [because] they were not bending to the will of a higher corporate power."

And as a songwriter who released her first album independently in 1999, Cook still holds tightly to that sense of creative freedom — both for herself and for fellow country artists.

"I feel like on the eighth day, when God made the internet — or maybe it was the 10th or 11th day — I'm so grateful because I feel like it has put power back in the hands of the people," she says. "There's more of a level playing field and opportunity for artists who don't bend to the will of corporate demands of how you should make music, how that music should sound, and what the message should be, [to] have a platform and an opportunity to get their music out in to the world."

Other musicians, like Whitey Morgan and newcomer Austin Lucas, believe outlaw country is most aligned with punk music these days. That independent spirit of printing fliers, sharing them with venues, and digitally releasing music — with or without the help of a record label — connects the outlaw spirit of the '70s with the current times.

"With the internet stuff, social media, bands can do all their own shit now. It's such a DIY vibe in all types of music that it fits that genre or label perfectly. That's how the whole thing started as, doing things without the need of major labels," says Morgan, whose group, Whitey Morgan and The 78's, released *Hard Times and White Lines* in October.

"It's more of an underground kind of thing I guess that's happening today, as opposed to back then where it was that these guys were on mainstream labels, but they decided to tell the mainstream labels that, 'This is how I'm going to do it or I'm not going to do it at all,'" he

CHAD COCHRAN

Linda Ortega

GRANT M. PURDY

Elizabeth Cook

Whitey Morgan

continues. "Whereas today, it's almost a punk rock vibe where it's coming up from underground and people are promoting themselves and if the shit's good, it'll eventually be heard."

Additionally, there's a particularly feminist streak that has helped outlaw country persevere. Cook, as well as Nikki Lane (the self-proclaimed "First Lady of Outlaw Country"), Margo Price, Lindi Ortega, and others have led this movement into the 21st century. Their independence, as well as their fierce ideals and fearless storytelling on taboo topics like gender-based pay inequality and body autonomy, have carried the outlaw ethos to new generations.

Ortega, who released her seventh album, *Liberty*, independently in March, especially values the musical freedom that comes with starting her own record label.

"I'm happy to be able to release on my own imprint, for sure," she says. "It's definitely because I wanted to do things my way and create the music I wanted to create without external forces trying to guide my music a certain way."

And while *Liberty* draws influences from spaghetti Westerns (a film genre she also connects to the outlaw spirit), she also cites Willie, Waylon, and others as musical heroes. And on her last EP, 2017's *Til the Goin' Gets Gone*, she even offers a haunting, pedal steel-heavy cover of Townes Van Zandt's "Waiting 'Round to Die."

Ortega's tie to outlaw country goes past the usual suspects, though. She likes to explore how other female country musicians in particular took those innovative, independent ideas and interpreted them on their own.

"I think there's an attitude about outlaw country music that I quite like: It goes against the grain. Especially in that era, I mean, Loretta Lynn could have even been considered an outlaw, too, based on the content of what she was writing about."

Name-dropping songs like "Fist City" and "The Pill," Ortega continues, "She doesn't often get cited along with them, but [Lynn] definitely was an outlaw. I think it's all about going against the grain of what was socially acceptable back in that era and rebelling against the

MICHAEL MESFOTO

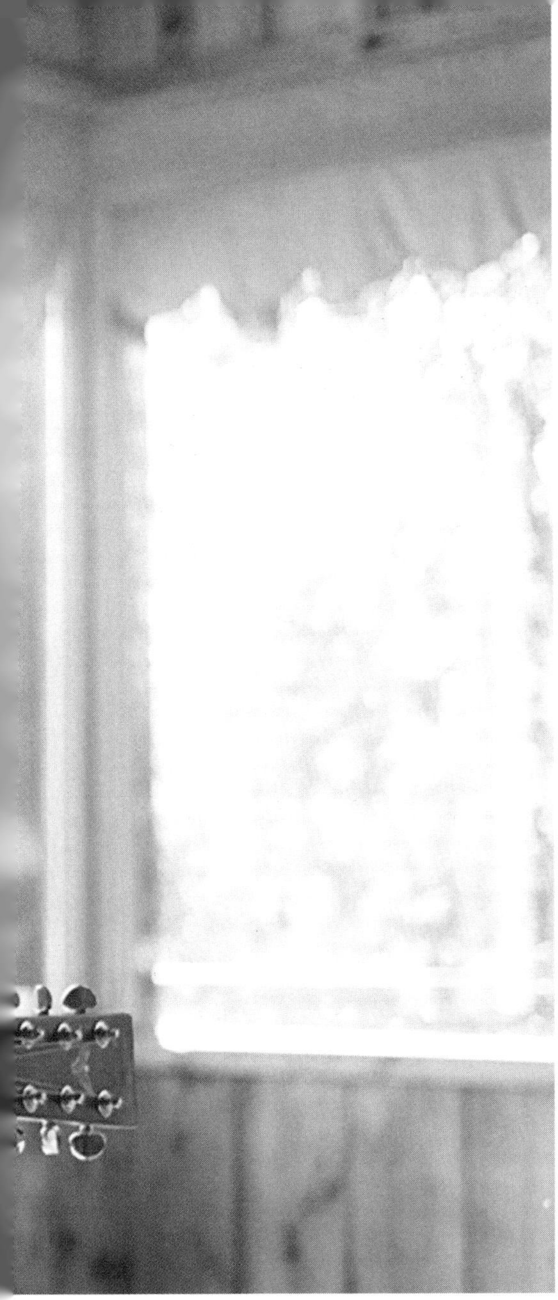

straight-and-narrow of the '40s and '50s."

But even as these and other DIY artists have channeled the spirit of the genre's founders, outlaw country music has seen its share of commercialism in this modern era. Capitalizing on the partying side of the outlaws, the fourth annual Outlaw Country Cruise will take place Jan. 27-Feb. 1, 2019, setting sail from Tampa through the Bahamas. Presented by Sixthman and Renegade Circus, the lineup includes artists like Steve Earle & The Dukes, Joe Ely, and Dale Watson & Lone Stars who, in the late-'70s and '80s, picked up where the outlaw originators left off; outlaw progeny (who have earned respect in their own right) like Shooter Jennings and Bobby Bare Jr.; alt-country stars like The Drive-by Truckers and Old 97's; as well as newcomer feminist outlaws like Cook, Price, and Lane.

It's a bonding experience for those aboard, gushes Cook, who has played all the Outlaw Country Cruises. And there's something to be said for uniting people who feel marginalized in any way, including for their taste in a strange sub-sect of country music.

Others, like Morgan, however, watch this cool factor manifest from afar via hip T-shirts and a ploy for likes on Instagram posts. He scoffs, "It kinda blows my mind how fucking hip it is to like Waylon and all these guys now."

Still, as the original outlaws established, it's both cool and innovative for musicians to have some say in their own musical output. In these times of independent production and releases and listener-based musical Darwinism, creative control is a vital part of the industry, especially in the historically inflexible style of country music.

Flippo, the Rolling Stone journalist whose old works helped inspire the *Outlaws & Armadillos* exhibit, also wrote the liner notes to the *Wanted! The Outlaws* compilation record in 1976. In those notes, he seemed to broaden the scope of outlaw country music even further: "Call them Outlaws, call them innovators, call them revolutionaries, call them what you will, they're just some damned fine people who are also some of the most gifted songwriters and singers anywhere." ■

IT'S HER WAY

A new biography celebrates the music and influence of Buffy Sainte-Marie

by Beverly Bryan

MATT BARNES

BUFFY SAINTE-MARIE, a new authorized biography of the '60s folk icon, presents an image of a wonderfully complex artist. It's a picture of a singer, songwriter, guitarist, and composer who has been making groundbreaking music since her 1964 debut with songs that have been both experimental and wildly popular. It's a picture, also, of a woman who has enjoyed a successful career, but for whom making music has always been just one way to speak her truth. Finally, it's an impassioned argument for Sainte-Marie as a talented and innovative musician whose work has too often been ignored, when it should be celebrated.

Sainte-Marie was born to Cree parents on an Indian reservation in Saskatchewan, but was adopted by an American family. Although she has lived and worked in the US almost her entire life, she is better known in Canada than she is in the United States. A major reason for this is that the US government blacklisted her from the radio in the late '60s and '70s for her politically outspoken music, which often focused on the rights of indigenous North Americans.

In a phone interview, Sainte-Marie reflected on the blacklisting era. "It was so strange in the '60s once blacklisting had started. My career was kind of nipped in the bud, and to just hear the comments of some other artists. Once I was gone, and a lot of other people were gone too, a lot of the originality disappeared from music at that time because of blacklisting, but nobody knows the stories."

Finding the Right Voice

Buffy Sainte-Marie's author, Andrea Warner, a Canadian music critic and assistant producer for the CBC Music radio network, noticed the inequity in the way the singer's music has been treated when she started focusing on Canadian artists in her journalism. Though Sainte-Marie has become a more familiar name in Canada, Warner found that she often isn't seen as being in the same league as the musicians who were her peers.

"I was really struck by how, even though she's a ubiquitous figure, she is very seldom spoken about with the same sort of reverence as Neil Young or Joni Mitchell or Leonard Cohen, and the more that I dug into her music, the more that I learned about her life, the more frustrated I got," Warner says. "This is such an incredible songwriter. The actual spectrum of her music is so diverse, so interesting, and so, I think, unknown to a lot of people. I was very frustrated that there was just not much attention paid to that and not much credit attributed to her. I thought she had been erased, particularly as a woman of color in Canada and an indigenous woman."

Sainte-Marie herself has turned down other would-be biographers, and just one other book on her life and work exists. That text, *It's My Way*, came out in 2012 and was written by historian and indigenous studies professor Blair Stonechild with Sainte-Marie's full participation. *It's My Way* is exquisitely detailed and gives near equal weight to Sainte-Marie's many accomplishments outside of music — from her visual art to her creation of the Nihewan Foundation, a nonprofit dedicated to promoting education within and about indigenous communities.

Still, *It's My Way* received mixed reviews. Pop culture writer Lindsay Zoladz praised *It's My Way* in the *Los Angeles Review of Books*, but also admitted to some disappointment. "I found myself wishing that it focused more closely on Sainte-Marie's music, that it was more forceful in arguing for her spot alongside Dylan and Cohen and Mitchell in the now-calcified countercultural canon that Sainte-Marie so rightfully deserves," she wrote.

Sainte-Marie says she accepted Warner's pitch for a new biography because the writer "writes like a girl, and I love that."

"I was really struck by how, even though she's a ubiquitous figure, she is very seldom spoken about with the same sort of reverence as Neil Young or Joni Mitchell or Leonard Cohen, and the more that I dug into her music, the more that I learned about her life, the more frustrated I got."

Andrea Warner

"[Warner] seemed to see the more expansive, deeper, sometimes softer focus than just, 'Get to the point. Tell us how much money you made and who you fucked,'" she says.

"I'm a biblioholic and I read all the time and I've read a lot of music biographies," she continues. "Andrea seemed to want to know different things. When she was writing about my mom she just seemed to pick up on some of the sweetnesses about my mom that maybe a different writer, a male writer, might not have even been interested in, even noticed. And my approach to the music, she would seem to see it in a more expansive way than just the typical music biographer would."

'Bottomless' Music

Warner describes Sainte-Marie's discography as "bottomless." Likewise, her influences run deep and encompass vast musical territories. Sainte-Marie's first musical loves ranged from Tchaikovsky to Elvis, and her eclectic tastes influenced both her vibrato-heavy vocal style and guitar playing, including but not limited to the traditional music of India (before George Harrison and The Beatles made it hip), flamenco, Edith Piaf, and very early blues and gospel.

It's also significant that Sainte-Marie is a self-taught guitarist with a preternatural gift for playing by ear who wrote using self-devised tunings. "When I first got a guitar I didn't have anybody to show me how to play it, so I didn't know you were supposed to tune it one way," she says. "Maybe a song that was sad, I would tune in a certain way; a song that was happy, I would tune in a certain way. I just fooled around with the tunings until it sounded like I liked it."

These tunings were an early influence on the music of Joni Mitchell, who wrote the book's foreword. The then-more-famous Sainte-Marie was an early supporter of Mitchell, carrying around her demo tape and covering her songs in an effort to get them heard.

Elaborating on Sainte-Marie's influence on Mitchell, Warner says, "I think that's pretty important because everyone talks about Joni as a guitarist and she takes up that space, which is not her fault at all. It's the fault of media that can only envision one woman belonging amongst 500 great men. But I think it eclipses Buffy a fair bit, because she's actually a really great guitarist and, I think, a really interesting guitarist."

Sainte-Marie's emotive performances and deft songcraft first led her to renown in New York City's East Village folk scene alongside Bob Dylan and Phil Ochs. Word of the young artist's arresting songs and dramatic stage presence spread quickly beyond the Village. By her early 20s, she had already found lasting success on an international stage.

That her fame has persisted is due in part to the diversity and quality of the catalog she went on to produce, innovating with each album. She has written folk originals that sound old as Arthurian legend and others, like "Cod'ine," that feel like lost blues classics. Her early protest songs, such as "Now That the Buffalo's Gone," have aged well, and, sadly, remain relevant. They stand alongside her equally indelible love songs such as "Until It's Time for You to Go." On *Illuminations*, her haunting 1969 psych-folk album, she notably made studio magic with vocal overdubbing and a relatively new instrument, the modular synthesizer. It remains a landmark with a cult following.

In later decades, Sainte-Marie continued to explore the possibilities of electronic music and break further musical ground in moves like sampling traditional powwow vocals for the song "Starwalker." Her recent albums, like 2015's *Power in the Blood*, have been critically acclaimed and lyrically potent, leaning into critiques of the military industrial complex and winning her a new generation of fans.

Of *Power in the Blood* Warner says, "It was radical and subversive and powerful, but it also felt really contemporary in a way that a lot of her peers haven't felt that contemporary and vital in a long time." Throughout the book, Warner presents Sainte-Marie this way, as an artist either at the forefront of things or well ahead of her time, and often succeeding artistically and commercially in the process, in spite of a music industry that rarely knew what to do with her.

Fighting to be Heard

Throughout her career, Sainte-Marie's musical contributions have been unfairly eclipsed, to use Warner's term. As a prime example, "Universal Soldier" was Sainte-Marie's protest song — inspired by US involvement in Vietnam and written while many people were still unaware of what was happening — but it was Scottish singer-songwriter Donovan who made it a hit when he recorded it in 1965.

Warner writes: "Suddenly, everyone was talking about 'Universal Soldier' as if Donovan had written it. When he covered 'Cod'ine' shortly thereafter, Sainte-Marie's authorship was erased yet again. To this day, there are numerous websites that credit him as the songwriter and it's blatant sexism that, 50 years later, this is still a common misconception."

In the next paragraph of the biography, Sainte-Marie is quoted as saying, "I still have people insist that Donovan wrote 'Universal Soldier' and 'Cod'ine.' I've had people actually confront me about it." Warner suggests that the persistence of this misconception "could be attributed to the inherent 'authority' that society gives to men's words" versus those of women.

The keen feminist and intersectional awareness that Warner brings to issues like these is one of the biggest strengths of the book. Neither biographer nor subject shies away from discussing the childhood sexual abuse, abusive relationships, and other emotional trauma that Sainte-Marie has lived though. Rather, Warner frames these experiences evenhandedly alongside other parts of Sainte-Marie's story, like her dedicated advocacy work, indigenous rights activism, and musical independence.

On Sainte-Marie's difficult and complicated childhood, Warner says, "It was really powerful for me to talk with her about how that informed the integrity with which she led the rest of her life. She's always had a deeply held sense of herself. She's always been able to turn inwards and replenish herself."

Warner's intimate storytelling and sensitive portrayal of her subject makes *Buffy Sainte-Marie* both an enjoyable read and a valuable addition to the literature about such an important artist. Fans of Sainte-Marie's work will especially relish the pains Warner has taken to secure the musician's legacy. By showing how Sainte-Marie has inspired generations with her creative genius and fearless truth-telling — even when she was systematically made invisible — Warner's biography helps write her back into the canon of musical innovators. ■

D. BRIAN CAMPBELL

The Mekons

DERRICK SANTINI

TWO WORLDS COLLIDING

Cowpunk and the move to alt-country and beyond

by Chris Parker

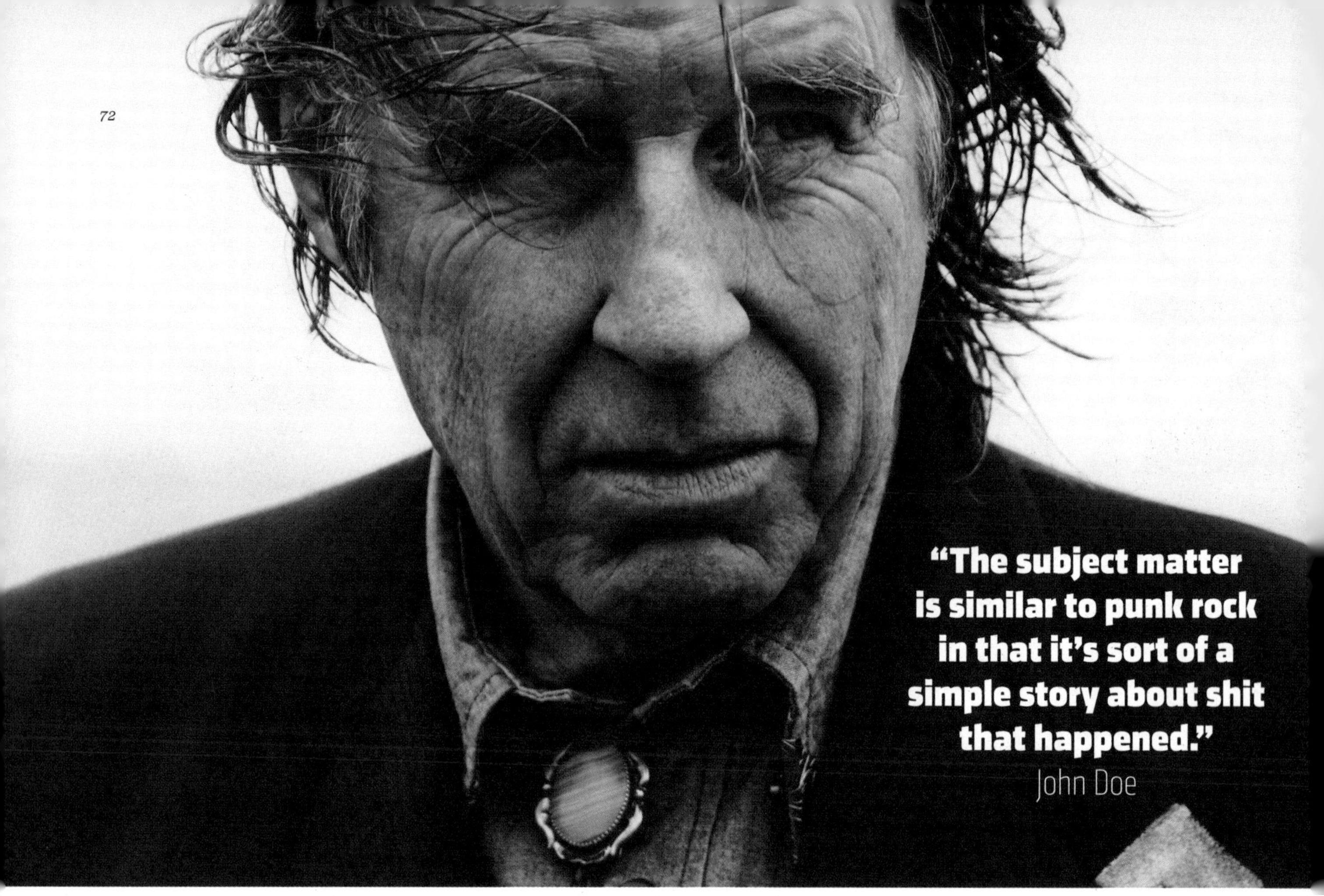
"The subject matter is similar to punk rock in that it's sort of a simple story about shit that happened."
John Doe

FOR DECADES, PUNK MUSIC has been described as urban folk. Its origins didn't represent a country-versus-city divide so much as a cultural malaise hovering over modern society. In its earliest days, punk encompassed an attitude as much as a musical style. But as the chunky downstrokes hastened and the backbeats pounded in time, musicians who grew up listening to other types of music cross-pollinated punk with their personal histories, borrowing and merging elements in new ways.

A key formative ingredient in California punk was the Bakersfield Sound, which emerged in the 1950s as a reaction to the slickly produced country music of the time, integrating rougher guitars, drums, and lyrics. The Bakersfield Sound — pioneered by artists such as Merle Haggard and Buck Owens — was too loud, open, and creatively aspirational for stodgy Nashville, but just right for a new audience.

"I interviewed Buck Owens one time and asked him the difference between West Coast country and back-east country, and he said it was belt-buckle polishing," recalls Dave Alvin, who founded The Blasters with his brother Phil in Downey, California, in 1978.

"Because of the social norms back east you couldn't grind into your dance partners' hips like you could on the West Coast," Alvin continues. "That created a different musical world and things were a touch more open minded."

But from the branch of the Bakersfield Sound in California, another subgenre began to splinter. Now known as cowpunk, it encompasses all types of rowdy rock and roll influenced as much by the country greats as by punk, garage rock, and new wave. Still, when The Blasters began, "cowpunk" hadn't yet been coined; it was all just punk.

Year-Zero Punks

Last June, Alvin released a record with Jimmie Dale Gilmore called *Downey to Lubbock* that was inspired by the music of Los Angeles' famed folk club The Ash Grove, where both saw bands in the early 1970s. Back then, the local honky-tonk jukeboxes featured songs from Merle Haggard right alongside those of Sam Cooke. That all-encompassing attitude played a role in the diversity and eclecticism of the early West Coast punk scene before it diverged into more formulaic hardcore.

"Everyone came to the punk rock scene and brought their own taste in music and what they grew up listening to," says Alvin, who grew up with a "big jumble of stuff" he heard on the radio, including country, R&B, and early rock, all of which found homes in The Blasters' sound.

West Coast punk rock found expression in a wide variety of approaches. "There were some parameters," Alvin says. "Inside those parameters it was pretty wide open."

On the other side of the globe, a group of art school kids in Leeds formed The Mekons after witnessing The Sex Pistols. When The Mekons' 1979 debut — full of avant-garde noise rock — went nowhere, they nearly broke up. Feeling washed up with nothing to lose, they

JIM HERRINGTON

recorded a country album.

"We were sort of year-zero punk rockers in 1977, coming around to this idea that maybe we were just a tiny little cog in the wheel, and we weren't destroying everything. Maybe there was this amazing tradition out there and we were somehow strangely part of it," recalls Mekons founder Jon Langford.

As X's 1980 debut *Los Angeles* pegged it, punk was "The Unheard Music." That early aggressive music covered the same ground as some country and folk music — tales of common people and life issues, honestly expressed without pretension or pomp.

"The subject matter is similar to punk rock in that it's sort of a simple story about shit that happened," says X's John Doe, who recently finished recording a new Flesh Eaters album with Alvin and project founder Chris D that's due out in 2019.

That common touch was a driving force for The Mekons, who had grown dissatisfied with the sloganeering and paint-by-numbers politics that they saw in punk at the time. Country's more provincial concerns offered a way out.

"We didn't want to be party political, we wanted to be 'the personal is political,'" explains Langford. "When I listen to [Johnny] Cash and Merle Haggard and people like that, it seemed what they were doing was describing real, everyday life. Punk was kind of an antidote to the progressive rock years of singing about hobbits and elves and stuff and trying to deal with real life, though a lot of the politics of punk rock was kind of macho fantasy as well."

A Growing Schism

While early Los Angeles trailblazers like X, The Blasters, Los Lobos, and Tex & The Horseheads always possessed a country sound, for others, including The Mekons, it became a way to remain punk rock once punk rock had lost its vibrancy. It's not that they didn't appreciate country music, but what they really loved was the opportunity to defy expectations.

"We were not averse to bucking the status quo even though we had plenty to do with establishing the status quo," says Chip Kinman, who, with his brother Tony, broke up California punk stalwarts The Dils in 1981 to start the country-rock band Rank and File with The Nuns' Alejandro Escovedo.

"We heard the power in Merle Haggard and Waylon Jennings; it was the same as punk rock, the same as Burning Spear. Of course we couldn't play reggae, but we could play country music," recalls Kinman. "It felt more like a mission than it was something new to do. It felt as much of a mission as punk rock did."

In fact, playing country music got Rank and File thrown out of punk clubs they'd packed years earlier. And when Meat Puppets toured with Black Flag in 1984, the audience's alienation was their per diem.

"After the show I would literally go and collect all the quarters that the fans had been throwing at us, and that's how I was eating on off-days," says Meat Puppets drummer Derrick Bostrom, who admits they courted danger with a no-fucks-given attitude that included playing everything from Rodgers & Hammerstein to Fleetwood Mac.

As subsects of punk like hardcore and cowpunk began to differentiate themselves throughout Los Angeles, the original scene began to fracture.

"There were a lot of great hardcore bands, but I lost interest in it as soon as it became apparent [that] it has to be this or it can't be that," says Alvin. "As soon as anything becomes cookie-cutter like that, I get bored."

Doe writes about this period in Los Angeles in his forthcoming book, *More Fun in the New World*, a collection of essays detailing punk rock between 1982 and 1987 that's due out next June. In one essay he writes: "There became a split somewhere in '82 or '83 between punk rock and hardcore; that is when I would say what became alt-country started happening."

Swings and Misses

Around the same time that Rank and File were getting started, Jason Ringenberg moved to Nashville, fortuitously settling into an apartment behind the only punk rock club, Cantrell's. He'd grown up on a farm in northwest Illinois equally impressed by country and punk. Ringenberg soon found his foil in guitarist Warner E. Hodges, helping turn the nascent Jason & The Scorchers into one of the hottest live acts of the era.

"He really loved first AC/DC, Van Halen, and Zeppelin much more than the Pistols and Hank Sr., which is where I was coming from, so there were a lot of arguments," Ringenberg says. "But the common ground was '50s country and '70s punk rock."

Their 1982 DIY debut EP, *Reckless Country Soul*, wet the whistle like top-shelf bourbon, sparking a million-dollar bidding war won by EMI. They followed the next year with the *Fervor* EP and then two LPs, 1985's *Lost & Found* and 1986's *Still Standing*. While the albums received great critical notices, they struggled commercially, in part due to limited radio airplay. They were too country for the rock stations and too rock for the country ones. Touring was difficult as well.

"It was a different scene than for West Coast bands. California's so big they can play there all the time, whereas

"We had a vision for what we were doing and we just kind of saw this opening that no one was doing and we ran in that direction. You didn't see anyone with tattoos and long hair that was clutching an acoustic guitar, banjo, or fiddle."

Danny Barnes

in the Midwest and the South it was scattered and you really had to get out and network and get to know people in different towns," Ringenberg recalls. "We were part of the R.E.M., Guadalcanal Diary, 10,000 Maniacs, Replacements-scene circuit with all those bands from the Midwest and the Southeast."

Lone Justice, led by the big voice of Maria McKee, was another young country-punk band that seemed destined for stardom. The half-sister of Love singer/guitarist Bryan MacLean, McKee spent her youth hobnobbing with Laurel Canyon musicians but was heavy into acting, and even considering applying to Juilliard, when the music bug hit hard, inspired in part by seeing Bruce Springsteen live.

Lone Justice's early demos showcase a white-hot act, but Jimmy Iovine, who produced their eponymous 1985 full-length debut, pushed them away from country toward a heartland rock sound. When the album didn't meet commercial expectations, McKee's band was fired and the process for her next album, 1986's *Shelter*, was micromanaged. Still young, McKee wasn't confident enough to push back, and she wound up demoralized, ending Lone Justice and leaving the country.

"For me it's like I was going through a phase where I was singing like Dolly Parton but I was this kid that grew up in like gothic, post-Doors Beverly Hills theater school," McKee explains, recalling drama classmates Nicolas Cage and Crispin Glover. "I was just kind of playing a character and I did it so well that it sort of defined me and chased me, though it couldn't be further from the truth. So I feel like I have been trying to outrun Lone Justice for decades."

Even Meat Puppets, while critically adored, were possibly shorted their due.

"There was a considerable gap between when we recorded [*Meat Puppets II*] and the time we could mix it, like maybe six or seven months," Bostrom says. "[It] came out in the spring of '84 and it did very well and it got a lot of credit. But it if had come out when it was supposed to we might have been the original country-punks."

A Second Wave

By the mid-1980s, that first wave of country-punk had dispersed. Dave Alvin left The Blasters in 1986. He replaced Billy Zoom in X for that year's *See How We Are*, then went solo when X broke up. The Kinmans lost interest in Rank and File and had moved on to other projects by 1988. In 1990, Jason & The Scorchers broke up. Cowpunk made way for alternative rock, which was about to step aside for grunge and indie rock.

By the time Meat Puppets made it to a major label, London Records, for 1991's *Forbidden Places*, it felt like low tide for cowpunk. "They got [Dwight Yoakam guitarist and producer] Pete Anderson to produce our record," Bostrom recalls. "About the time that record came out, Nirvana happened and the label's like, 'Shit, we miscalculated.'"

Yet even as grunge overran the music scene like dandelion seeds, country-punk's strains had already taken wind,

finding another generation of musicians to take up the cause. In Austin, Danny Barnes formed the trio Bad Livers, inspired by the country music of his youth, the punk of his teens, and unclassifiable weirdos like The Butthole Surfers. (Surfers guitarist Paul Leary even produced their first album, 1982's *Delusions of Banjer*.) Their bluegrass-punk sound was a cultural blender, by design. They might cover Mississippi John Hurt or Motörhead, fueled by Barnes' furious banjo.

"We had a vision for what we were doing and we just kind of saw this opening that no one was doing and we ran in that direction," Barnes says. "You didn't see anyone with tattoos and long hair that was clutching an acoustic guitar, banjo, or fiddle. Not like only a few, absolutely zero."

Not one to stand still, Barnes added tuba and accordion to the fiddle/banjo/upright bass lineup. Like the first wave of cowpunk, there was a self-conscious desire to push and challenge the audience. (Barnes is still challenging folks with his most recent project, last year's *Stove Up*, his first all-acoustic banjo album that's also an homage to Don Stover.)

"We felt we had a real mission to turn people on to different things," says Barnes. "We were turning traditional people on to weirder music and... [other] people onto Johnny Cash, Ralph Stanley, and stuff like that."

In the Midwest, The Bottle Rockets' Brian Henneman had picked up a guitar after punk gave him the notion that he could make music. By the time he'd figured his way around the instrument,

The Bottle Rockets

CARY HORTON

Lucero

Henneman had found his main inspirations a little outside the genre, taking a cue from Jason & The Scorchers and building upon the country rock he loved growing up, like The Marshall Tucker Band and Lynyrd Skynyrd.

"I had the skill and right at that time is when I discovered Jason & The Scorchers," says Henneman, who recently finished a new Bottle Rockets album, *Bit Logic*, that came out in October. "It was like the perfect storm, right there. They were doing the guitar rock but it was country and punk rock. Around the same time I discovered Steve Earle and it was really those two that pushed me out the door."

Living in the tiny town of Festus, Missouri, Henneman got to know the neighboring bands, including a trio called The Primitives from across the river in Belleville, Illinois. Henneman's band at the time, Chicken Truck, played shows with them in the mid-'80s. (Parents had to drive The Primitives to the gigs because they weren't old enough yet.)

By 1988, The Primitives had become Uncle Tupelo, and they invited Henneman along on tour when they got signed. They even got him a deal for The Bottle Rockets' first album, and when Henneman initially didn't have a name for the band, his buddies suggested it.

"It was [Uncle Tupelo's] manager, Tony Margherita, who got me a record deal off of some goof-ass demos we did while they were recording their second album," Henneman recalls. "I was happy being their auxiliary guy. Then he got me a record deal [for 1992's self-titled debut] and I had to throw a band together. The whole thing worked ass-backwards."

In the late-'90s, bands like Ben Nichols and his band Lucero — which released its ninth studio album, *Among the Ghosts*, in August — started going against the grain. Like Rank and File they started by pissing off their punk rock friends with an earnest stab at country.

DAN BALL

"My life would've been a lot easier if I had just played punk rock songs at punk rock shows or country songs at country shows, but no ... we chose the most difficult path," admits Nichols with a laugh. "We've always had that rebellious streak in us, I guess."

They were clueless to their antecedents. "We didn't even know who Uncle Tupelo were when we started the band," he confesses. But their impulses were pure.

"I was like, 'I want to do a band that's kind of like Johnny Cash mixed with The Pogues.' I thought it was something new, but no," Nichols says, laughing again. "Then you try to find your niche and carve out your spot in that pantheon ... we're not inventing anything new with what we do, just trying to write some good songs."

Around the same time that Lucero was first coming to life in Memphis, a powerful Irish-punk act was making its start in a Los Angeles bar. Flogging Molly put their own twist on something old made new again.

Flogging Molly leader Dave King admired how The Pogues blended loud guitars with traditional music and made it sound like a natural fit. "They influenced us all in the music that we did, but there was never really electric guitar like that before," says King. "I think ourselves and The Dropkick Murphys stepped that up a bit. But done in a way that it's still beautifully married."

Common Ground

King feels like merging modern and traditional sounds — whether you call it cowpunk, folk-punk, or alt-country — makes perfect sense.

"To me they're one and the same, just different clothing," he says. These styles of music, no matter where they come from, share an energy "that goes beyond amplifiers and amplification."

Cowpunk can cover so much territory because it's an authentic expression of something humans shared at one time or another — a longing for community and connection, even if they're perhaps looking for one that is a bit beyond social norms. And in that kinship, there's an acknowledgement of similarity across time. ■

TECHNOLOGY MEETS TRADITION

Inside the making of Wilco's 'Yankee Hotel Foxtrot'

by Will Hodge

"Being a really insatiable music fan, I'm really well versed in song forms and musical traditions, but I don't get excited when I make that thing. I always feel the itch to subvert those forms so that I can hear something special in what I'm doing."

Jeff Tweedy

NOT MANY ALBUMS COME prepackaged with their own multilayered mythos, but that's just one way among many that Wilco's iconic fourth album, *Yankee Hotel Foxtrot*, broke free of rules and expectations. Even before the album was officially released in stores on April 23, 2002, its complicated origin story had played out for months via interviews, magazine articles, blog posts, and any other medium covering music news. The loss and replacement of band members, record label disputes, intra-band creative turmoil, "now or never" pressures, early online self-distributed streaming innovations, unintentional connections to the 9/11 tragedy the year before, and the unique situation of being dropped by a label and then essentially being re-signed by the same label through a subsidiary are just a few of the unorthodox narrative threads tied to this significant album. To add another interesting layer to the legend, by an incredible stroke of serendipity the vast majority of these storylines were captured as they transpired and packaged into an intimately shot behind-the-scenes documentary by Sam Jones called *I Am Trying To Break Your Heart*.

While there's no denying that all of these extraneous plot points contributed to the pre-release buzz surrounding *Yankee Hotel Foxtrot*, the album has stood on its own creative merit since its highly anticipated release. "If you're talking about Wilco with someone and you're trying to explain what makes the band unique and why they're important, *Yankee Hotel Foxtrot* is the record that most people would bring up first," states Steven Hyden, music journalist and author of *Your Favorite Band is Killing Me* and this year's *Twilight of the Gods*. "It has all the elements of classic American songwriting and there's also an undeniable sense of futurism to it. They took the dustiness of American folk music and twisted it and subverted it with technology."

SAM JONES

Jeff Tweedy during *Yankee Hotel Foxtrot*-era rehearsals

Amid all the dramatics around the writing, recording, and releasing of *Yankee Hotel Foxtrot*, sometimes the stories at the heart of the album — the 11 painstakingly crafted songs themselves — can get lost. However, strip away all of the storylines and the music itself stands as one of the most powerful and significant albums of the 21st century. *Yankee Hotel Foxtrot* is the soundtrack of a band essentially dismantling and recontextualizing folk music for a new millennium by employing an array of technological devices meant to highlight the obstacles in basic communication and understanding.

There's a tense scene in the *I Am Trying To Break Your Heart* documentary that seems to articulate this enigmatic dissertation on communication that plays out both musically and lyrically throughout *Yankee Hotel Foxtrot*. During the grainy, black-and-white scene, Wilco frontman Jeff Tweedy and multi-instrumentalist/co-engineer Jay Bennett are having an increasingly pained discussion about the way a song transition should be mixed, and it's clear that the actual content of what they are saying to each other has taken a back seat to the larger context of the dynamics within their strained relationship. Even if casual music fans may not understand the nuances of what it means to "go offline and unmute everything to find out what track that thing's on" or to "mix to the edit instead of making a new edit," it's plain to see that what they're talking about isn't really what they're talking about. After a decision forward is somewhat agreed upon, conversational gridlock immediately ensues again as Bennett's desire to autopsy their previous exchange is quickly rebuffed by Tweedy's incensed pragmatism.

With his head in his hands, Bennett pushes, "I just want you to understand me." Tweedy exasperatedly interrupts, "Why is that so important? I don't have to understand you all the time. It's okay. We found it and we can do it." Bennett, unwilling to let things lie, passive-aggressively concedes, "Okay, it just seems to me like you're making a big deal out of not wanting to understand me." As their verbal sparring continues, both men move farther away from the camera while another out-of-frame conversation starts closer in. The resulting effect makes it increasingly difficult to hear their conversation while also adding an additional layer of unsettledness to the scene, as what the audience sees (the visuals of one conversation) does not match what the audience hears (the audio of a second conversation). And then an unrelated acoustic blues number comes in from out of nowhere to underscore the whole scene and muddy it further.

Subverting the Form

Ruminating on the writing and recording of *Yankee Hotel Foxtrot* from the kitchen table of Wilco's Willy Wonka-esque Chicago wonderland known as The Loft on a midweek afternoon, Tweedy says that his original vision for the album may have been unintentionally embodied in that agitated scene from the documentary. It's a microcosm of the album's larger thesis: "I think the description I would've used at the time to convey what I was hoping to achieve with *Yankee Hotel Foxtrot* is like when you put on a record at home and it doesn't have the emotional impact that you want it to because you intentionally chose it, you physically put it on, and you anticipate what's going to happen. You're asking too much of it. However, if you walk into a bar where there's a jukebox playing and there are people talking and all these other noises are going on, you have to fight your hearing and your consciousness to really make out what's playing. I've always been so much more drawn to that type of stuff than anything else. I've always thought that type of experience was special because it becomes more of a transmission from a further away place."

Throughout *Yankee Hotel Foxtrot*, Tweedy addresses that idea of otherworldly transmissions — along with the associated themes of connection, distance, miscommunication, disorientation, etc. — in a variety of unconventional ways, both lyrically and musically. To achieve this, he focused not just on the obvious practicalities that go into making an album (what is being played and sung), but also in the indiscernible processes of the songwriting and recording phases. "I spend as much time reading experimental poetry and literature as I do listening to music because I'm really fascinated by process," Tweedy says.

Around the writing and recording of

Yankee Hotel Foxtrot, Tweedy was digging into writers like Gertrude Stein, but not for their writings as much as for their philosophies. "After language has been used for so many hundreds of years, how do you get someone to see a rose again? How do you describe it?" ponders Tweedy, referencing Stein's iconic "Rose is a rose is a rose" line from her 1913 poem "Sacred Emily." Acknowledging his tendency to easily become bored with his own work, Tweedy continues, "I wanted to see how I could dismantle language and sound so that they would become exciting again."

The fact that Tweedy is completely uninterested in retreading the same creative ground can easily be seen in the sonic evolution of Wilco's catalog. Formed from the ashes of pioneering alt-country band Uncle Tupelo, Wilco recorded three full-length albums prior to *Yankee Hotel Foxtrot* — 1995's *A.M.*, 1996's *Being There*, and 1999's *Summerteeth*. Hyden summarizes that trio thusly: "*A.M.* is essentially an Uncle Tupelo record without Jay Farrar, *Being There* is when they started establishing their own identity as a band, and *Summerteeth* is the most dominatingly Jay Bennett-sounding record."

Since their inception in the mid-'90s, Wilco has made albums that each have built upon the success of the previous one, and the band quickly became indie rock heroes thanks to their willingness to take risks and grow their sound into more expansive sonic territories. Tweedy says the band's continued maturation grew out of a "constant innate restlessness" within himself: "Being a really insatiable music fan, I'm really well versed in song forms and musical traditions, but I don't get excited when I make that thing. I always feel the itch to subvert those forms so that I can hear something special in what I'm doing.

"Over time, the same chords tend to go together," Tweedy continues. "I can't really do much to change that, musically speaking, but I knew I could make those traditional forms fight through something to become more valuable."

To create the tension and struggle felt throughout *Yankee Hotel Foxtrot*, Tweedy leaned heavily on an inanimate co-conspirator: technology. Many of the foundational elements of Wilco's sonic arsenal are present on *Yankee Hotel Foxtrot* — gently strummed acoustics, twangy rock guitars, big drums, a broad range of pianos and synthesizers — but there are a variety of other, unconventional sonic elements (detuned radio signals, static-filled droning, kaleidoscopic splashes of indecipherable feedback, a loop of a phonetic alphabet broadcast, chiming bells, backwards tape loops) meant to create a layer of disconnection and confusion between the song and the listener. As David Fricke described it in his 2002 *Rolling Stone* review of the album, "There is genuine bedlam here ... the enchanting sound of things falling apart."

Sometimes those chaotic electronic atmospherics were employed directly, such as the heavily distorted hiss swirling around the tape loop of "I'm the Man Who Loves You" that plays at the end of "I Am Trying To Break Your Heart" or the static Morse code loop running underneath "Poor Places." Other times technology was employed in the form of actual devices used to affect the sound of something else, such as an electronic egg whisk whirling across guitar strings in "Poor Places" or the Korg Kaoss Pad pitch-bending various signals and frequencies throughout the last minute of "Ashes of American Flags." For Tweedy, the inclusion of these electronically manipulated elements into the traditional Wilco sound was more ornamental than transformative: "It always bothered me that people would say it was experimental. It was experimental to us, but it certainly wasn't something that hadn't already been conducted in modern music. We were discovering new things for ourselves, but it was still rock music rooted in traditional folk and country songwriting."

The interesting relationship between the band's conventional instrumentation and their tech-infused curiosities is eloquently addressed in a beautifully edited segment in *I Am Trying to Break Your Heart*. For the scene, shots of the band casually running through the chord changes of "Poor Places" on just two acoustic guitars, a hollow body bass, one hand drum, and a shaker are juxtaposed against Bennett and drummer Glenn Kotche showing off some of the more eccentric sonic and rhythmic ingredients that appear on the final track. Bennett's voiceover states, "A lot of times when you're playing, if you don't have any sonic landscape behind you, everything turns into a folk song. We just wanted it to not sound like a little folk ditty. We wanted to have some sonic weight under all of that."

Giving some additional context to some of the odder technological apparatus on display in the scene, Tweedy says, "One night we gave ourselves an assignment for everybody to make something that would be a self-playing musical station. The idea was that we would turn it all on in the morning and just record it. We did the same thing again on our next album [*A Ghost Is Born*] on 'Less Than You Think' by using things that would play by themselves and also evolve over time. Like a fan blowing on something that's not sturdy enough to continue functioning the same way or plugging into a guitar pedal that would morph the sounds over multiple repetitions, like glacial changes."

In his 2004 *The New York Times* book review of Greg Kot's Wilco biography *Learning How To Die*, writer Joe Klein describes the give-and-take between music and technology on *Yankee Hotel Foxtrot* opener "I Am Trying To Break Your Heart" by saying: "Tweedy sings the words tentatively, from a distance ... backed by free-range clanging and scraping, the melody overwhelmed by electronic anarchy." He later applauds the way that the tradition-meets-technology approach umbrellas over the entire album: "It skates the border of brilliance and pretense, filled with memorable songs that are constantly subverted, or perhaps augmented, by electronic mayhem."

Source Material

Perhaps the most notable nonmusical moment on *Yankee Hotel Foxtrot* is the one that ended up giving the album its title. Around the 3:49 mark of "Poor Places," a hauntingly robotic female voice starts flatly repeating the three words beneath the musical bed of lead vocals, mix-metered drumming, guitar-and-piano interplay, and increasingly erratic atmospherics. The cold refrain repeats unwaveringly for a full minute and a half as the song descends into squalls of guitar feedback contrasting against a continuous single-chord piano thump. The source material for the unsettling sample is *The Conet Project*, a box set of CDs that contain recordings from numbers stations, fascinatingly mysterious shortwave radio broadcasts that are believed to be used by government agencies to communicate with active spies out in the field.

Tweedy picked up his copy of *The Conet Project* on a whim while wandering the aisles of a Tower Records in Chicago one day because he thought it looked interesting. A longtime fan of quirky field recordings, his inclination toward the album makes sense. As Tweedy recalls, "When I was a kid, one of my favorite records in my dad's collection was an old Folkways record of train sounds. I think it was called *Sounds of Steam Locomotives* and there were several volumes of it. My dad worked on the railroad for 46 years and that's the only reason I think he had it. That's my first memory of something like that, but it really sparked my interest in field recordings. Later on, my brother had a record by Manfred Mann's Earth Band called *The Good Earth* that started off with a rooster crowing. I'm fascinated with stuff like that, so *The Conet Project* was right in my wheelhouse."

Tweedy put *The Conet Project* recordings to use in his deconstructed songwriting process. He would drive around and try to sing the songs he was working on over the numbers station recordings. "It felt really uncomfortable to me in a good way," Tweedy says with a laugh. When the band starting constructing "Poor Places" in the studio, Tweedy remembered the icy female voice from the track named "Phonetic Alphabet – NATO" and tried it out in the mix. "It was so unsettling by itself, but the disembodied woman's voice felt appropriate for the song," he recalls. "There is a ton of stuff like that on the record where we would be listening to a mix and then throw on a whole different element to see what would happen. We would put sounds on top of other sounds and sit and listen because something would always happen. Eventually you'd

"There's a feeling of disconnection and dislocation in a lot of the songs that highlight the modern conundrum with technology — the paradox that we have more ways than ever to connect and yet it seems like it's harder than ever to get your point across."
Steven Hyden

either get annoyed with it or it would stick and become a part of what we were working on in a way that you couldn't take it away."

The idea of writing a song and then using technology to shift fearlessly around its sonic foundations stretched throughout the writing and recording process for *Yankee Hotel Foxtrot*, often resulting in markedly different versions of the same song and an exorbitant amount of electronically enhanced overdubs from which to pick and choose. In fact, the "more is more" approach grew so exponentially that Tweedy eventually brought in Chicago-based experimental musician-producer Jim O'Rourke to help sort through everything and strip away any excesses during the album's final stages. To get a song where he wanted it to be, Tweedy would often try multiple approaches, sometimes using only the lyrics or a vocal melody to act as an anchor around which everything else could be swapped in and out: "I was writing songs and putting ornate chords in them and then pulling them back out and seeing if I could sing the same song with only one or two chords. I would ask myself, 'How few chords can I use to get this song across?' That developed all the way into things like 'Poor Places' and 'I Am Trying to Break Your Heart,' where there's a drone going through the whole thing. I would see if the songs could still land if they were sung over just one note or one atmospheric element."

Showing, Not Telling

For all the work that Wilco put into musically deconstructing their folk-rock tendencies and building intentional sonic barriers of entry for listeners to navigate, the album's lyrics were equally labored over to make sure the payoff would be worth the struggle. Tweedy intentionally tinkered with conventional syntax and grammatical structures to convey the ease with which miscommunication breakdowns can happen, and he drew on the inspiration of Stein to come up with a fresh new approach to language and lyrical interplay. "I was trying to do the same thing with the lyrics that we were doing with the music," he says. "I was trying to make new connections between verbs and nouns that you don't normally associate with each other. We get so used to using the same verbs with the same nouns. They tend to pair up over time."

For an example of Tweedy's verbal vandalism, look no further than the album's very first line, in which he croons "I am an American aquarium drinker / I assassin down the avenue." While the unorthodox placing of a noun where a verb should be isn't brand new on its own, the brazen utilization of it as the album's lyrical introduction (especially when placed within the song's dizzying sonic landscape) sets the proper expectation that audiences are in for an "all bets are off" experience. Klein even went so far as to say that "the use of 'assassin' as a verb is, I think, as pure an expression of rock 'n' roll's outlaw sensibility as you are likely to find."

In addition to its musical role, technology plays a prominent role in *Yankee Hotel Foxtrot*'s lyrics as well. Not only does Tweedy sprinkle in references to machines (ATM, radio, phone, camera, typewriter) throughout the songs, but the themes of disconnection and miscommunication can easily be seen as commentary on the discussions that were being had around the time of the album's release (and still today) about technology and how it affects our relationships and the ways we interact with each other. As Hyden puts it, "There's a feeling of disconnection and dislocation in a lot of the songs that highlight the modern conundrum with technology — the paradox that we have more ways than ever to connect and yet it seems like it's harder than ever to get your point across."

This conflict is wonderfully highlighted in the song "Ashes of American Flags," where the opening verse's detail of the song narrator's prosaic human-to-machine interaction ("The cash machine is blue and green for a hundred in 20s and a small service fee") contrasts sharply with a later verse's distressed human-to-human one ("I'm down on my hands and knees every time the doorbell rings"). The song's poetic

Yankee Hotel Foxtrot tapes

MARK GREENBERG

analysis of connection and communication skews even blurrier when the chorus states "All my lies are always wishes," which is later tweaked to "All my lies are only wishes." With falsehoods and untruths (unintentional or not) representing some of the biggest obstacles to communication, it's notable that Tweedy also includes the concept of lying in the lyrics to "Kamera" ("Which lies I've been hiding") and twice in album closer "Reservations" ("I've always told lies for love" and "The truth proves it's beautiful to lie").

"It's one thing to write a song about how you can't communicate with someone," Hyden says. "It's another thing to make a song actually sound and feel like a breakdown in communication. It's the difference between showing and telling. I feel like *Yankee Hotel Foxtrot* is more about showing you than it is about telling you what the songs are about."

'Noncommercial' Nature

Apart from the role it played in the music and lyrics of *Yankee Hotel Foxtrot*, technology has also heavily impacted some of the logistical issues surrounding the album, namely its original (non-physical) streaming release in the fall of 2001, as well as the possibility of it ever properly being remixed or remastered in the future. When Wilco originally handed in the finished version of *Yankee Hotel Foxtrot* to its record label, Reprise Records bristled at its "noncommercial" nature and eventually dropped the band without releasing the album. However, in an unusual turn in the music industry, Reprise gave Wilco the rights to the album as they shopped it around to other labels. Before eventually signing with Nonesuch Records, the band made *Yankee Hotel Foxtrot* available to stream for free via their website, a distribution option that was still in its infancy in 2001, when the words "free online music" were synonymous with illegal music piracy and peer-to-peer file sharing networks. Instead of having an adverse affect on the physical sales of *Yankee Hotel Foxtrot*, the album sold more than 55,000 copies in its first week and landed at No. 13 on the Billboard 200 album chart. So far, *Yankee Hotel Foxtrot* is still the only Wilco release to have achieved gold selling status.

As far as the potential for any reissue of *Yankee Hotel Foxtrot*, the normal expectations of an album getting remixed (adjusting how the individual sonic components relate to each other within individual songs) and remastered (adjusting how the overall album sounds by aligning the individual song mixes with each other) may be impossible to meet due to how the songs were originally recorded, mixed, and pieced together.

"It's all from so many different sources and stored in different places. I'm not even sure if it technically could be done," Tweedy acknowledges. Many of the album's tracks were recorded on older ADAT (Alesis Digital Audio Tape) and 2-inch tape machines, mixes were bounced between 24-track and 48-track consoles, some sources were converted over to 1/2-inch tape for stereo mixes, and then most of the final mastering was done after everything was formatted to DAT (Digital Audio Tape) processing. The use of so many different recording machines and mediums, as well as the additional elements that were added or tweaked at various stages, were combined effectively enough to craft one of the most singularly adventurous albums of the 21st century. However, the Frankenstein-like process the band employed means that reverse engineering it back down to its individual analog components for remixing and remastering isn't something that fans should expect anytime soon, or maybe even at all.

However, there is one option Wilco could explore for an eventual *Yankee Hotel Foxtrot* reissue of grand proportions that would probably contribute to the album's mythos in even deeper ways. Because of the process by which the album was written, recorded, mixed, remixed, broken apart, and pieced back together in different ways — and because of the extended time period when the finished album was stuck in label limbo — multiple alternate versions of the album's tracks and songs that didn't make the final cut exist and have found their way to fans through digitally bootlegged sources. For Hyden, the option of compiling all of the "officially unreleased" material into one cohesive project would be more than well received: "I'm fascinated by all of the different versions of the *Yankee Hotel Foxtrot* songs that are out there and the way they allow listeners to track their evolutions. There's great potential for a *Yankee Hotel Foxtrot* box set that captures those alternate arrangements and the other recorded songs that aren't on the album and puts them all in one place."

Lasting Transmission

As Tweedy looks back over the process by which *Yankee Hotel Foxtrot* came to be, there's a bittersweet tone to the way he moves between discussing the creating versus the creation: "To be honest with you, I was pretty frustrated with everything up until I talked Jim O'Rourke into helping me put it all together. I was pretty frustrated at trying to get at something that just felt so elusive."

That elusiveness, the idea of blending technology with tradition to create something that somehow felt both authentically old and completely new, while daunting in its pursuit, proved revelatory in its fulfillment. By taking those risks and braving the unforeseen gauntlet of what the entire *Yankee Hotel Foxtrot* era turned out to be, Wilco managed to make good on their desires to be true to themselves, their goals, and their thirst for sonic adventure. Tweedy acknowledges that this was achieved through a combination of following some creative instincts while continually fighting others: "By taking field recordings and radio broadcasts and layering them over the fairly simple rock music that we were making, we were hoping for something exciting to happen. We ended up being blown away by those moments of recognition that something random happened that was way better than what we had intended to do. You can put the guitar solo on the track that you know will work because you've listened to a thousand Beatles songs or you can surprise yourself."

By using technology to push for such constructed-yet-randomized magic, Wilco ended up with its signature album — one that just so happens to have also become one of the landmark albums of this century. "*Yankee Hotel Foxtrot* seems ancient and futurist at the same time," Hyden says. "It's a version of Americana that doesn't seem sepia-tinged. It's 21st-century folk music."

Tweedy mostly talks about the album in more personal terms: "It sounds kind of naïve and silly to say in hindsight, but it was exciting and it didn't hurt anybody. It was a fun way to make our music more exciting to ourselves."

With *Yankee Hotel Foxtrot*, the statement is firmly made that technology is as much a means of connection and clarity as it is a means of obstruction and interruption. Looking to deconstruct what it meant to write folk songs and what it meant for them to be received by listeners, Wilco used technology as a fully realized musical instrument in the same way they used guitar, bass, piano, or drums. By masterfully evoking the idea of disconnection — both sonically and rhetorically — and creating intentional barriers of discomfort and discord, Wilco managed to connect with audiences more deeply and on a wider scale than they previously had. Though they may never be able to summon the exact set of circumstances that led to the creation of *Yankee Hotel Foxtrot*, by Wilco standards that is more than an acceptable trade-off. As long as audiences continue to lean in, listen closely, and keep their antennas up and moving, those otherworldly transmissions will be there — broadcasting, repeating, and waiting to be received. ■

THIS THING'S ON

Ear Trumpet Labs creates mics with meaning

by Allison Hussey

EAR TRUMPET LABS

Ned Luberecki

MOST MUSIC FANS CAN'T rattle off all of the equipment their favorite artist uses; the amplifiers, microphones, and all the attendant stands and cables are merely accessories to the main attraction. But there are some pieces of gear whose appearances command a second look, like microphones that appear to have time-hopped to the stage from the early 1940s. A casual listener may not immediately be able to hear a difference, but they can at least see it: Bands gather around these modern-built but retro-looking mics to sing and play together. For a growing coalition of musicians, they make a world of difference in conveying the best sound they can possibly deliver.

Those bespoke microphones are the work of Philip Graham, who runs Ear Trumpet Labs in Portland, Oregon. Since 2011, he's built gear that has earned adoration from rockers like Elvis Costello and The Decemberists, bluegrass elder statesman Del McCoury, and many more artists in many more genres.

Graham has taken an unusual path to making these beloved condenser microphones — mics that are more technically and electrically complex than their basic modern counterparts, but produce more natural sounds. He was previously a software programmer, but as he grew more and more tired of his day job, he turned his attention in his leisure time toward tinkering. He built pinhole cameras and tube amps, and when his singer-songwriter daughter became interested in recording, Graham taught himself how to build microphones.

"I was getting increasingly frustrated with programming, and just kind of reached a snapping point with my job," he says. "I just kind of up and quit, and then was sort of looking around like, 'Well, what can I do now? I have these weird microphones that I've been building, and people seem to like them, so maybe that's a business.'"

At first, Graham was looking to develop an excellent condenser microphone that would be used as a studio mic. But from some of his musician friends, he realized that in live settings, acoustic musicians were using gear designed for loud rock music. Microphones meant to convey the bombast of a squealing electric guitar at high volume won't always meet the needs of a quiet acoustic artist. It's the gear equivalent of trying to eat soup with a fork.

"My design attention was on satisfying that problem, of making the best kind of acoustic sound [so] that people wouldn't have to use pickups in their acoustic instruments, and to get a kind of vocal quality that I'm pretty convinced you can only really get if you give a little distance from the mic," Graham says. "The vocal instrument

SHELLY SWANGER

Andra Day

actually resonates over a fairly large part of your body, and close mic-ing that — literally from a couple of centimeters off of your lips — is no different than jamming a microphone an inch from the face of a guitar. It's going to sound terrible, and you're really not capturing the full sound of the instrument."

The distance principle of Ear Trumpet mics also means that musicians have to stay a little more aware as they're playing.

That translates into musicians doing a little mixing of themselves live by moving closer to or farther away from the mic as they play, which some musicians, including mandolin maven Sierra Hull, enjoy.

"It's really fun to kind of be a little more in control of [your] dynamic versus having somebody at the sound board turning you up and down and riding your solos, if you're just plugged in or using a clip-on microphone or something," she says.

Edwina and Friends

Graham essentially stumbled into his microphones' distinct visual aesthetic by way of his tinkering. He was building his first microphones from pieces he found in his basement or in hardware stores, like shiny copper pipe. Simultaneously inspired by the aesthetics of the industrial design boom of the 1930s and '40s, Graham realized he could make a product that looked as special as it sounded. He gave his earliest models what he calls "old lady" names — Josephine, Edna, Edwina — and it all just stuck.

Graham found early Ear Trumpet devotees in Portland's Foghorn String Band, friends of his who fell in love with the Edwina model and took it out on the road.

"That first couple of years, they basically built the company," he says. "Everywhere that they went on tour, I'd get calls the next day. I could tell exactly where they were going on tour. I'd get calls from the sound guy, and I'd get a call from a couple of people that had just seen them."

Audiences for old-time and stringband shows are frequently made up of other musicians, which fueled interest in Ear Trumpet far outside Portland. Word began spreading about these special microphones.

"It's a great marketing demonstration every time any artist uses them," Graham says with a laugh. That was true for Hull: After embarking on a duo tour with singer-songwriter and former Della Mae guitarist Courtney Hartman, who brought along her Edwina, Hull bought an Edwina and a Louise of her own.

Soon, Graham had made fans out of The Milk Carton Kids, whose delicate acoustic songs necessitate a crisp clarity in a live setting. Within a couple of years, celebrated Dobro player Jerry Douglas had gotten wind of Ear Trumpet Labs,

COURTESY OF EAR TRUMPET LABS

Del McCoury

too, and got a mic of his own. That snowballed into Graham outfitting one of Douglas's many projects, the Flatt & Scruggs tribute act The Earls of Leicester, with a full complement of microphones. As the bluegrass community fawned over the Earls, it took note of the band's mics, too.

"The thing is, in the bluegrass community, they all talk to each other. Word spread really fast there," Graham says. "As soon as people see somebody of that caliber that thinks that something works for them, they're certainly willing to give it a try."

Once the bluegrass community found something that worked for them, they latched on tight, Graham says. He posits that his wares fill a void in that music that other microphones simply weren't meeting.

"I think they've just been frustrated for a long time and have been wanting something that's designed to work well live. There haven't been a lot of great options for people. They'd been trying to use studio mics for ages and really wanting to do a single mic or minimal-mic setup, and just not had any good options," Graham says.

On Stage, In Studio

Of course, a handcrafted piece of music equipment doesn't come cheap: A new Ear Trumpet Lab mic ranges anywhere from $550 for the Chantelle, Edna, or Edwina models to $1,200 for an Evelyn or a Mabel. A custom setup costs even more. (But artists on a tight budget can turn to certified resellers that stock used devices at a lower rate.) Even for up-and-coming bands, an Ear Trumpet mic can be a worthwhile investment toward getting new ears to tune in.

Steph Stewart fronts Blue Cactus, a country band based in Carrboro, North Carolina; prior to that outfit, she led Steph Stewart and The Boyfriends with guitarist and now-partner Mario Arnez. Stewart and The Boyfriends had tried a condenser microphone from another company, but found that it was a little too finicky, and the band struggled with feedback at shows. Arnez did some more research and found Ear Trumpet Labs, eventually settling on an Edwina.

Because Graham had originally imagined his microphones as studio tools, they work just as well for recording as they do on stage. For Stewart and Arnez, having the Edwina means that they can make quality recordings of material they're working on.

"When we do demos, we plug it in to Mario's computer, which has all of the recording equipment on it. We can record live that way, just duet demos, and get really good sound quality for a simple setup. It's so versatile," she says.

As Graham has grown Ear Trumpet Labs, he's added more models to his lineup, like the Nadine, which is designed specifically for an upright

COURTESY OF EAR TRUMPET LABS

Becky Buller

bass. He's thrilled that the company has been able to grow to the point that it has — Ear Trumpet Labs has a staff of five, including Graham, and a steady stream of business — but unlimited expansion isn't the goal. That's part of the appeal for artists like Hull.

"You know you're supporting this small, personal company of this group of folks that are hand-making these things. That's kind of cool as well, rather than just not really knowing where your microphone comes from," she says, adding, "It's pretty cool to know that there's a lot of love and care that goes in to building these things."

That type of rabid support from performers, who place trust in the equipment's story as well as its craftsmanship, is what puts Ear Trumpet Labs' mics at the top of performers' wish lists. But Graham doesn't want to get production to a point where he has to forgo the careful making of every microphone. Don't expect to see a massive factory line of Ear Trumpet mics hitting the shelves at big-box music retailers any time soon. That dedication to quality control and attention to detail has helped Graham corner the market. As musicians around the globe keep singing the brand's praises, Ear Trumpet Labs makes sure that audiences hear every note. ■

SHELLY SWANGER

UNDER A (VIRTUAL) TREE

Online lessons and tools connect music students and teachers like never before

by Stacy Chandler

AFTER A LITTLE CHITCHAT about school and a recent music festival, 14-year-old Gracie Mae Grossman and International Bluegrass Music Association fiddle award winner Becky Buller get down to business at a recent lesson — the business of "Uncle Pen."

Buller plays through the song as Gracie listens intently, watching Buller's bow and fingerings. Then Buller talks through the kickoff, explaining different ways people might do it at jams. She plays a phrase or two, slowed down. Gracie plays back each phrase on her fiddle, and from 450 miles away, she starts to get the hang of it.

The lesson isn't knee-to-knee, as countless fiddle players in previous generations learned the song, but rather screen-to-screen, allowing Buller in Manchester, Tennessee, and Gracie in Huntington, Indiana, to connect and make music together.

This kind of connection — students to their musical heroes, musicians to another source of income in a tough business — happens across state lines, national borders, time zones, and hemispheres. The internet, along with high-speed connections and apps that enable reliable video and audio exchange, has broken down barriers like time and distance between students and teachers, allowing songs to be swapped and relationships to form between people who a couple decades ago would have been unlikely to even meet.

Learning's New Frontier

Becky Buller has been teaching music lessons since college in the late 1990s. Back then, it was a way to fulfill a full-time work requirement to get in-state tuition at East Tennessee State University, along with work-study in the school's Archives of Appalachia and a job at a gas station. But she also enjoys teaching, and a couple of years ago she started adding online lessons, via Skype or FaceTime, to her mix of students, who range from elementary school children to retirees.

There's not much difference, she says, between the lessons she teaches in her home and the lessons she conducts online. Students, for the most part, choose the songs they want to work on, and Buller breaks each song down and works on the skills needed to play it, emphasizing learning by ear.

"Let's just take it note by note," she says of her online approach, "like we're sitting under a shade tree and I'm teaching you this tune – of course, it's under a virtual tree – and we'll go through it bit by bit and I'll try to go as slow as I can. I always try to figure out better ways to show people stuff or explain stuff if they start looking cross-eyed. That's the same as a lesson here at the house."

But some things, of course, are different. An online lesson can be recorded, allowing the student to refer back to key moments. Because audio over internet connections tends to be a one-way street, playing together is hard to do, and student and teacher have to be careful not to talk over each other, Buller says. They both also have to make sure their hands stay within camera range — it's easy to drift off the screen, meaning one may miss what the other's fingers or bow is doing. Eye contact can get a little weird, as anyone who's been in a video conference can attest, because it feels more natural to look at images on a screen than directly into your computer or phone's camera. And there are some hands-on aspects of teaching that get

CAITLIN MCDONAGH

lost in online translation.

"Every so often it's a little frustrating to not be in the room with the student so I can just, like, move their hand, if they're having a positioning issue or something," Buller says. "Or if there's something just technical on their fiddle that I can quickly fix for them, that's a little hard, to have to send them off to a luthier, especially if I'm not familiar with the area and I don't know who to send them to."

But talking them through such issues can help a student think about them on their own, Buller suggests. "I want to teach them to fish, I want them not to be completely dependent on me," she says. "It forces me to get more creative with how to get them to fish when it's long distance. It's good for me as a teacher. It stretches me."

She also wants her students to play for and with other people. She holds a public recital each year, with even some online students traveling to Manchester to take part. And much of her teaching addresses how to play in a jam setting, which students, including Gracie, do regularly, often sending videos to their teacher as proof of progress made.

"I try to encourage them to get involved in their musical community. Find a jam session, find a youth orchestra, find a camp," says Buller, who has used the internet and social media to help find local resources for her online students. "It's so important to play with other people."

Expanded Options

Online lessons are just one option the internet has opened up for students with an instrument in their hand and the desire to figure out what to do with it. YouTube offers instructional videos on any instrument you can imagine, as well as easy access to live performances from which a student might be able to glean technique, style, or fingerings.

Websites like Banjo Hangout (and counterparts for fiddle, Dobro, guitar, and mandolin) host forums where players of all skill levels can talk shop and exchange videos, and visitors can also find links to lessons on DVD and books from established publishers like Homespun and Mel Bay. More recently, new websites have sprung up with the express purpose of connecting high-profile performers with students — for a fee.

ArtistWorks, founded by a jazz guitar-playing former AOL executive who couldn't find a teacher to work with where he lived, offers subscribers video lesson libraries from big-name teachers in a range of genres, including Bryan Sutton on guitar, the Infamous Stringdusters' Andy Hall on Dobro, Missy Raines on bass, Tony Trischka on banjo, and Mike Marshall on mandolin. Students can submit videos of their practice to their teacher for personalized feedback, and all videos and feedback are accessible to other subscribers in case they might be struggling with the same issue.

Peghead Nation similarly offers subscription-based video lessons, with an emphasis on roots music. Its String School instructors include Bruce Molsky, Brittany Haas, Mike Compton, Bill Evans, and Joe K. Walsh.

For mandolinist Walsh, who is also an assistant professor in the string department at Berklee College of Music in Boston, Peghead Nation is just one of many teaching venues. He travels frequently to instructional camps, and it was one such event in Canada's remote Yukon region, where there aren't a lot of options for mandolin instruction, that got him thinking about online lessons.

In addition to a few students he gained after visits to the Yukon, he has also taught students from all over the United States, one from Lebanon, and a business traveler who often connects with him from China. (For comparison, a student in England, an Amish girl in Indiana, and a truck driver who logs in from stops along the road have been on Buller's student roster.)

With online learning as an option, Walsh says, "a student has access to people with knowledge that they may not find in their community. You have access to people who have spent such a huge amount of time focusing on their instrument. And that was impossible before on any realistic level before for most students. That's a huge transforming element of this."

Teachers, too, are able to broaden their reach, with new ways to fit instruction into lives already busy with touring, performing, writing, and recording.

"I have a few hundred students on Peghead," says Walsh, "and there's no way that I could reasonably find time for all those students in my schedule. But with online learning I'm able to share some of what I've learned with a greater number of students than was previously physically possible, and the students have access to the person who they really would like to learn from and sound like. So that's the huge, huge upside."

In the roots music world, online learning has a practical advantage too — an added revenue stream that helps musicians make ends meet. That's no small thing, says Buller. "The internet has ... made it easy to get lessons from professionals in the industry, and it helps the professionals, because bluegrass is still a relatively small genre, so this helps us to keep the lights on. It's really helping both the professionals and the students in a way that just a few years ago would be completely unthinkable."

Camp Camaraderie

Just as passing along songs knee-to-knee has been part of the roots music tradition, camps offering intensive group work in music are part of the learning experience of many musicians, both hobbyists, as students, and professionals, as instructors.

But even camp may be finding a home online. Last June, North Carolina singer-songwriter Jonathan Byrd hosted an online songwriting retreat. Over the course of a weekend (including Friday evening), Byrd led eight students through writing exercises, discussions, group and one-on-one feedback, critique, and performances. The students, from several US states, Canada, and the UK, logged into the retreat via video conferencing app Zoom at scheduled times, with time to work on their songs independently offline between sessions.

Byrd had the idea for an online camp after attending an in-person one that required him as well as the students to travel, in some cases long distances.

"Those are great, they're really powerful," he says. "It's good to get away from home and get away from everybody you know and your routine and really immerse yourself into something. But it's also really expensive and time-consuming and inefficient, as far as the environment and fuel is concerned."

He admits he had some worries about whether the camp vibe would translate online, but says he was pleasantly surprised. "You have this screen, and to keep weird audio effects from happening you have to have headphones on. So it feels like it's going to be like making love in a spacesuit, kind of, but it works. Once you start talking about ideas and once you start feeling the passion that everybody feels for wanting to do this thing and the commitment that they've made, it really works."

Being online required some workarounds, he says. Technical issues made one student miss a one-on-one session (Byrd says they were able to make do over email), and instead of a live concert he had to pre-record some songs he wanted to play for his students. But the online camp also added some instructional tools: an immediate group visit to YouTube to watch videos of songs that came up in conversation, a virtual whiteboard where ideas could be collected for everyone to see.

Everything's Accessible

For students at every level, the internet has opened up a treasure chest of tools to help them learn the basics, play like their heroes, or simply conquer "Uncle Pen" or any other favorite song. "Everything's accessible, there are more resources now for a learner than ever before," says Walsh. "If a student wants to learn, say, a Chris Thile tune, it's much easier than it would have been 30 years ago."

He cites modestly priced resources like the Amazing Slow Downer and Transcribe! apps that can help musicians play along with a song in a different key, or make a loop of tricky parts of songs, slow them down, and replay them in a way that can untangle what's hard to make sense of at full speed. Backing tracks help players simulate playing with others, giving them the confidence to play a break when their turn comes in a real-life jam.

But there's one thing that all these online tools haven't changed, any teacher will tell you: You've got to be willing to learn, and you've got to put in the time and the work. You can watch YouTube videos all day, but if you don't pick up your instrument and play along, if you don't really dive into that kickoff to "Uncle Pen" and play it again and again, faster and faster, until you've got it deep inside your body and your brain, you might as well be watching cat videos. You also have to take charge of your own instruction, finding ways to meet your evolving needs as you progress.

"I think the most crucial aspect is a student has to be willing to self-evaluate with honesty, and that hasn't changed with the medium. That's still the constant," Walsh says. "The people who are best have figured out how to do that in a way that's both honest and doesn't totally capsize their morale." ■

SIDE HUSTLE

Artists have always had to hustle — both in and out of their creative pursuits — to make a living. Even Renaissance-era musicians, painters, sculptors, and others had to work outside of their artistic pursuits in order to find patrons who would support them. The process has changed over the past 600 years or so, and the modern musician's hustle manifests in many ways. The cliché, of course, paints performers as the baristas and bartenders who save enough money by day to chase their dreams by night. And while this tried-and-true tactic is still popular and effective, some musicians lean on technology to create part-time jobs like coding or accounting that can be done from the road. Others utilize their musical talents offstage by making and selling their own instruments. An even smaller group has found additional creative-based work to help subsidize life as a professional musician. We've highlighted six roots musicians who have used their extra-musical ingenuity to find six innovative ways to sustain a career in this field.

— Hilary Saunders

Charlie Overbey of Lone Hawk Hats

PHOTO COURTESY OF HONEYWOOD VINTAGE

LONE HAWK HATS

I've been playing, recording, and touring for too many years to count. I read somewhere recently that out of $43 billion made in the music business each year, just 12% goes to musicians [according to a 2018 Citigroup report], and that's mostly from touring.

Let's face it: Very few people are making a living from creating music. There's a lot of great songs out there, but artists these days have to have another outlet or "shtick" to stay afloat.

I've loved and worn hats in all of my lifetimes and stages of musical growth. I've always loved the exploration of finding them and of reshaping them to my liking. It was a natural progression for me to dig even deeper and start making and selling them with a bit of a nudge from my better half and partner Vanessa Dingwell. Her own company, Honeywood Vintage, is what I credit largely for the inspiration for really going for it with Lone Hawk Hats.

While juggling my own music career, I've been lucky enough to make hats for a large crowd of amazing music folks from Blackberry Smoke to Nils Lofgren of the E Street Band, Kesha, Dickey and Duane Betts, Elizabeth Cook, Chris Shiflett of Foo Fighters, Lenny Kravitz's guitar player Craig Ross, Marcus King, Adam Slack of The Struts, Aaron Lee Tasjan, Natalie Bergman of Wild Belle, Brian Venable of Lucero, and more. Lone Hawk Hats was even heavily featured in a recent Stella McCartney campaign.

Aside from building valued friendships, my hats have opened doors for me from touring to radio, and even some upcoming film and television placements. Most musical success these days is unfortunately not just about talent and songcraft, but about connections, contacts, and that extra something that sets you apart from everyone else. Lone Hawk Hats has done that for me.

— Charlie Overbey

PHOTO COUTESY OF HONEYWOOD VINTAGE

NELL ROBINSON

BANJO BOY COFFEE

The idea for Banjo Boy Coffee came about when I was touring with John Reischman and The Jaybirds. The bassist, Trisha Gagnon, supplements her road sales by selling homemade jam, which she does quite well. I was trying to think of ways the rest of the band could generate sales, I came up with the idea of Banjo Boy Coffee after talking with Jaybirds banjo player Nick Hornbuckle, who is a coffee roaster. I nabbed the URL banjoboycoffee.com and my partner Nell Robinson suggested I use a great Bay Area roaster with a long family history in the coffee business.

Next came Deering Banjo. Since I was playing their Solana six-string banjo in shows, they asked me if I would do custom blends for them. We spent a couple months tasting and blending coffees.

Now we have Banjo Boy Six String, Five String, Four String, and Ukulele blend coffees all inspired by Deering banjos and sold by the Nell & Jim Band at shows as well as via Deering Banjo Company online.

The coffee package reads "Wake Up to Good Music at nellandjim.com." We have a close relationship with a fan who is the owner of Sourdough Solutions in Colfax, California, and who sells Banjo Boy Coffee in the café. In addition, Banjo Boy Coffee offers sponsorships to select festivals, including the Old Settler's Music Festival, Bill Evans' Banjo Extravaganza, and the McCloud Bluegrass Festival.

We are really proud of these exceptional coffees and enjoy sharing them with folks who come to our shows.

— Jim Nunally

JAM'N MUSIC

Award winning musician and jam artisan Trisha Gagnon has been blessed with a wonderful and inspiring life at her British Columbia organic farm. "There's a little white house where the green fields grow," she sings in her song "Home Sweet Home" (co-penned with band leader John Reischman).

"I've lived in that little farm house for over 30 years," she says. "It's where I've written all of my songs, and harvested and produced my jams. Every morning, I wake up and thank God for this beautiful place ... for my good health, and so many blessings ... And then the day's work begins."

Singing, playing bass, and songwriting is Gagnon's first passion. She began performing with her sister, Cathy Anne McClintock, in the popular British Columbia band Tumbleweed in 1989, and for the past 20 years she's worked almost exclusively with John Reischman and The Jaybirds.

Growing organic fruit and making the most delicious jams is passion number two. And since winning the 2011 "World Jampionships" in the UK for raspberry jam, Gagnon's small home business has blown up.

"The balance between touring and my jam business can be challenging, especially when it's harvesting season. It's basically a one-woman operation! Since 2011 I've had to plant more and more fruit to keep up with demand. But with my dear neighbor Ria's help, we've been able to get everything picked before the possums can get to it."

If you catch Gagnon in concert with The Jaybirds, you may have an opportunity to bring home a jar of her amazing jam, which is also sold at farmers markets and events in British Columbia.

Both CDs and jam are also online at facebook.com/jamnmusic.

— Greg Spatz, The Jaybirds

PHOTOS COURTESY OF TRISHA GAGNON

JAM'N MUSIC
WWW.TRISHAGAGNON.COM
STRAWBERRY JAM
ORGANICALLY GROWN
Ingredients; Organic Strawberries,sugar,pectin,coconut oil
Need More Jam 604 793-4199
JAM'N MUSIC
WWW.TRISHAGAGNON.COM
APRICOT JAM
ORGANICALLY GROWN
Ingredients; Organic Apricots,sugar,pectin,coconut oil
Need More Jam 604 793-4199
JAM'N MUSIC
WWW.TRISHAGAGNON.COM
BLACKBERRY JAM
ORGANICALLY GROWN
Ingredients;Organically grown Blackberries,sugar,pectin
coconut oil
Need More Jam 604 793-4199

Trisha Gagnon's
jam 'n music
WORLD JAMPION
Raspberry Jam Artisan
Perthshire Scotland 2011
LOVE TO EAT
The World...
Jampionships™
WINNER 2011
WINNER!
"WORLD'S BEST JAM"
Perthshire, Scotland
Trisha Gagnon's
jam 'n music
CD Release
www.trishagagnon.com

THE MURAL SHOP

In 2000 I graduated with a BFA from the University of North Carolina and immediately took an apprenticeship with a muralist in my town. I was playing drums and touring with my band Dynamite Brothers at the time, so it was easy for me to work a little, go on the road for a while, then come home and work. It was very flexible. In 2003 I decided to strike out on my own and started my own business, The Mural Shop. Right about that time or shortly thereafter I also began playing drums with Birds of Avalon.

Birds of Avalon toured very heavily from 2005-10 and I was constantly trying to balance being on the road and coming home for small jobs here and there. I would take on anything from sketching elevations to painting fairies on kid's bedrooms to wayfinding signs in parking decks. Every so often I would get a mural gig. Over the next 10 years, I was able to build up a portfolio and client list that helped me earn more and more work.

Today, I am a full-time commercial muralist and sign painter. But I also continue to play music regularly. Birds of Avalon just released an album last year and Dynamite Brothers put out a new one two months ago. I can't say it is always easy to balance work and play, and I also have a 7-year-old daughter who is the number-one priority, but so far I have managed to make it work somehow.

— Scott Nurkin

RAIN BENNETT

HIGH CLASS HILLBILLY

When I moved to Nashville from New York to pursue music, I knew I would need to supplement my income. After 10 years in retail, the easiest solution seemed to be buying and reselling old cowboy boots and leather goods, and thus High Class Hillbilly was born. I wasn't sure how long I would be able to sustain juggling the two, but it seemed as my career in music grew, so did the supporters of our little vintage shop. Now I'm being asked to bring High Class Hillbilly along to festivals, and even to curate my own marketplace at Stagecoach each year.

For me, it's all about the hunt. It's truly one of my favorite things to do — wander aimlessly through a flea market or antique mall looking for things to clean up and either hold onto or resell. I believe it goes hand in hand with being a songwriter and performer, because the lifestyle and outfits that I bring onstage are those that have been carefully collected and nurtured, mile after mile ... just like the songs I hope to continue to write.

I'm very grateful to get to continue doing both jobs in tandem.

— Nikki Lane

BROOKE HAMILTON

WILLIE WATSON MFG. CO.

Being the skinniest person I know led me to start sewing about 15 years ago. It was out of necessity and I've always been the guy who's gonna "DIY" if I think I can pull it off. First I just started altering trousers and shirts. Taking in outseams and sleeves to get things to fit like I thought they should. It was fun so I figured why not just start from scratch. I got good at it and made a lot of pants, jackets, and a few dresses for my now ex-wife. Altering store-bought patterns and failing, the pants and jackets started piling up in the closet until they finally started looking right.

At the time, Old Crow Medicine Show was preparing to record our second record, *Big Iron World*, and we all came together to talk about it and share songs we'd been writing or working on. Everyone had songs and ideas to offer — old tunes to rework or new ones that needed lyrics. I had some tailored pants. So, I quit sewing all together for the next 10 years to focus on the band's career.

Fast forward to 2011 and I'm "just" a folksinger, not even trying to write songs. I was listening to Blind Willie McTell for three hours at a time, trying to hear something that might work for me to sing. I needed something to do while digging through these old songs, so I got out the sewing machine and made a shirt. It was awful and the topstitching was all over the place, but it was gratifying and I managed to start hearing the music again

EMILIA PARÉ

as I sewed.

Eventually, the music and sewing started inspiring each other. My shirts looked legit, but it wasn't until I made my daughter a certain dress (which turned into the "Polly Anne") that I thought maybe I would have something unique and worthwhile to offer. I made an Instagram page and sold a few, but I wanted to do more. I'd made myself plenty of jeans, and seeing that there really wasn't anything out there on the market that was truly equivalent to the many high end men's denim companies, it was a no-brainer to come up with a woman's cut. I've never been happier with anything I've designed than the lot — the 607 (named after the area code where I grew up), the 707, and the forthcoming straight/boot cut 615. People still don't quite believe or understand that I sew 100% of every garment myself, but I can assure you fine folks that I put a little love into every stitch.

— Willie Watson

WEARING THE PANTS

An all-woman mariachi group reinvigorates the genre

by Bonnie Stiernberg

CARLY ZAVALA

"We didn't think that a lot of our decisions were gonna create so much controversy ... like the wearing our pants, it's a big deal still, and the way we wear our hair and the songs that we choose to cover, the traditional people get offended or they don't like it or they don't think we're a mariachi group."

Mireya Ramos

WHEN MIREYA RAMOS went up to receive her Grammy last year, she had a vision.

"Sometimes you just see your life pass by," she says. "Like when you're going up to get the Grammy and say your speech, you just see all those 10 years of work that you've done and everything that went wrong and everything that went right. You think about that, and it's so many emotions at the same time. It's beautiful."

Ramos and the other members of Mariachi Flor de Toloache, the all-woman mariachi group she founded, took home the award for Best Ranchera/Mariachi Music Album for their 2017 record, *Las Caras Lindas*, becoming the first female group to win in the category. For a band that has innovated the genre by defying certain traditions and incorporating modern influences, it was validation.

"It's great that we get that kind of support from such a prestigious academy," Ramos says. "It was a huge breakthrough. It meant a lot."

That kind of support hasn't always been easy to come by for Flor de Toloache — particularly from purists, who have criticized the women's decision to wear pants instead of the traditional skirts worn by female mariachis.

"We ended up having to make [our outfits] ourselves, and that's how we ended up using pants and then making our own designs and kind of playing around with the mariachi traditional uniform," Ramos explains. "And that was important to us because I had a lot of experiences that were not always that positive in terms of like the culture clash and also the machismo that's very present in the industry, but also in the genre of mariachi, and I didn't come from that. All the women in my family are very strong, and at times I would express myself and some of the men would get offended and I just couldn't understand why."

Creating her own mariachi group allowed her to express herself, to challenge norms that go much deeper than fashion, and to reshape the music for a modern era.

"Staying with a traditional group, I wasn't gonna be able to compose my own songs and arrangements and all that stuff, so I just wanted a little more freedom. We didn't think that a lot of our decisions were gonna create so much controversy ... like the wearing our pants, it's a big deal still, and the way we wear our hair and the songs that we choose to cover, the traditional people get offended or they don't like it or they don't think we're a mariachi group."

Ramos, who grew up watching her father sing in a mariachi band, was also motivated by a desire to collaborate with more female musicians after coming up in a genre dominated primarily by men.

"The idea came through the whole experience of playing with male mariachis in New York, as I was one of the only females playing in the mariachi scene in New York, and I had seen where there were a lot of female mariachi groups in the West Coast and in Mexico, and I just couldn't believe that there wasn't one in New York, being such a big city and progressive," she says. "I knew that it was gonna be a big thing and some big part of the history, and it was exciting. It was an exciting idea.

"I also wanted to share my network that I had already created — not just the mariachi, but I was hustling in the city playing in a lot of different bands, and I met a lot of people doing that, and I wanted to share that network with other female players and I wanted the opportunity to meet other female players and collaborate with them and create a safe space where we could make music with no judgment and no obstacles we had to deal with as women."

Part of the Culture

Her first call was to Cuban-American singer-songwriter Shae Fiol, who was eager to join despite the fact that she didn't have much exposure to mariachi music at the time.

"I had never really listened to mariachi specifically at all, and the day that Mireya asked if I wanted to embark on this project and journey with her, it was totally new to me," Fiol says. "But I was like, 'Sure, let's do it!' So I just started listening to it, really."

Fiol's tastes had always leaned more toward pop, R&B, hip-hop, jazz, and folk. But with help from Ramos and others, she made a mariachi playlist and dove into its history and contemporary iterations.

"Really what struck me the most first and foremost as a singer was just the vocal style," Fiol says. "I was like, 'Wow, these are all singers that really can sing, sing, sing.' And I wanted to be able to do that."

She also picked up on the music's cultural relevance — its presence at major life events like birthdays, quinceañeras, and other celebrations. And that passion became personal.

"Just pride in it being Mexican and then it spreads all throughout Latin America, so to me it was just like, 'Wow, this is a really powerful genre of music that's actually really a part of the culture.' And I learned a little bit about my own culture, because my grandmother and my dad were both fans of mariachi and I had no idea, and they're Cuban, so I was like, 'This really reaches a lot of people everywhere in the world.'"

Mariachi Flor de Toloache's demographics reflect a similar diversity: The rotating collective of band members' backgrounds include Mexico, Puerto Rico, the Dominican Republic, Cuba, Australia, Colombia, Germany, Italy, and the United States, and as a result, their sound is a melting pot of influences that includes everything from cumbia to pop and jazz.

"Part of what makes Mireya and I so compatible is we both come from mixed backgrounds in our family, and so instantly you're kind of drawn to other people who have that same kind of thing going on," Fiol says. "Not exclusively, but it kind of happens naturally. And with that, just between the two of us, the range of music that we played and that we grew up listening to was so vast, and I think people with kind of mixed backgrounds, they're just exposed to it early, so it just comes out so naturally in our compositions and when we play. ... We like to incorporate those sounds because it's true to who we are as musicians, and so we let it come out. We let the jazz come out or let the rock or hip-hop or classical influences come out and encourage it. So while within the structure of a traditional sound, which we also love, we allow spaces for those influences from each member to come through, and it just makes it so special and unique and authentic to who we are."

It shouldn't come as a surprise, then, that the group has a collaboration with R&B superstar Miguel due this fall, and that their new album, which they were in the process of writing this summer, will feature appearances from other guest artists as well as more original songs. Ultimately, their goal is to push the genre forward and give young Latino fans a chance to reconnect to their culture.

"I think people have said a lot — and this is what I always appreciate — is there's a need for or a space for mariachi to grow, and that they feel like this could be what mariachi needs to stay relevant, and so they hear our music and they hear a lot of fresh sound to it because it incorporates stuff that's newer, stuff that younger folks are listening to," Fiol says. "So to take it and do it differently, some people hate it and some people are like, 'Oh, I feel like I can connect with it now.' People feel like they can connect to their culture again. For young people that are here or maybe even young people that are in Latin America, they're like, 'Oh, this is cool now. I can identify with it. I see myself in this. I hear myself in it.' " ■

LOOPS AND LEAPS

Gaelynn Lea approaches music on her own terms

by Robert Ham

MARK BROWN

THE VIDEO THAT SINGER-songwriter Gaelynn Lea submitted in 2016 to the panel of judges choosing the winner of NPR's Tiny Desk Contest starts off with a close-up of her left hand. Her hand moves up and down the neck of a violin as a miniature Orange amplifier that rests next to her whirs with the music coursing through it.

The droning melody she plays, calling to mind the decades-old folk of G.B. Grayson or the slow burn of Dirty Three, is doubled and trebled, a chorus of one instrument aided by a looping pedal. The shot stays relatively still for a full minute, then zooms out as Lea starts singing the first lines of her tender song: "Our love's a complex vintage wine / All ragged leaves and lemon rind."

When Lea finally comes into view, everything about the scene goes wonderfully against expectation. For one, it's the way she's playing the violin. It sits vertically next to her like a cello, held up by her left hand as she runs a small bass bow across the strings with her right. But mostly the pleasant surprise comes from seeing Lea herself.

She's sitting comfortably in a wheelchair, with one of her shortened legs tucked underneath her and her blue dress. Her arms are small and bent at unusual angles, all the result of being born with osteogenesis imperfecta, or brittle bone disease. The effect is a small shock to the system that quickly gets washed away once the swell of emotion that is her love ballad "Someday We'll Linger In The Sun" continues.

That reaction has spread widely in the two years since she and a friend filmed that clip on an iPhone. It won her the contest, earning Lea the right to perform a Tiny Desk Concert and accolades from judges like *All Songs Considered* co-host Bob Boilen and Black Keys member Dan Auerbach. That four-song set in NPR's offices has been viewed on YouTube more than a million times and completely altered the trajectory of her life.

"They took us on this five-city tour," Lea remembers, speaking from her home in Duluth, Minnesota. "After the first date in New York City, I remember thinking on the plane, 'I could totally see doing that more but I'm not going to ask my husband to quit his job.' But we started talking about if we could see ourselves touring for real, and we agreed that we could. Now we work together and live together and travel everywhere. It's really cool, but very different from where we started off."

Making It Work

Lea has spent all of her life taking bold leaps of faith like that. As a fourth grader, she decided she wanted to join the school orchestra, not concerned in the least about the fact that her arms make it impossible to hold most instruments the "normal" way.

"I told my mom that, and she said,

'Well, I'm sure you'll find a way to make it work,' " Lea recalls. "And I was lucky enough to have a teacher that was open-minded enough to adapt with me."

For this, Lea had to tap into her spirit of innovation, choosing to play the violin even though she was unable to tuck it under her chin and couldn't use all the fingers on her left hand. She started playing in the style of a cello, using a pen cap stuck to the bottom of the instrument to keep it from slipping. It took her no time to flourish with it, tackling tricky pieces by Beethoven and folk fiddling alike, as well as teaching others how to play.

Lea also started performing throughout her hometown, finding welcome collaborators in the local folk scene as well as a more high profile supporter in Alan Sparhawk of Low. The fellow Minnesotan heard her playing at a farmer's market with musician Charlie Parr and became so enamored with her sound that he started texting her, asking to collaborate. Lea and Sparhawk soon started writing and performing together around Duluth under the name Murder of Crows, and he even joined her during her Tiny Desk Concert, playing guitar and providing backup vocals on two songs.

"It was really amazing to see," Sparhawk marvels about her NPR appearance. "The whole company was there when she did her session. For weeks prior, everybody had been falling in love with her and her music. ... It's really the perfect kind of exposure, the perfect step off for her."

Sparhawk recognized that talent early on, encouraging Lea's first songwriting efforts, but the major contribution that he made to her work was gifting her the amp and the loop pedal that she used in her contest video. Despite her protestations, he insisted that she was going to like it and that she'd eventually start playing shows on her own.

"I didn't believe it, but he was right," Lea says. "I tried it a couple of weeks later, late at night, and I remember creating this symphony of sound and being like, 'Oh my goodness, this is a game changer.' I texted him at 1 in the morning, sending him a clip of what I had made."

From that point, Lea's career moved calmly and steadily forward. She played plenty of gigs around Duluth and self-released a handful of recordings, including the hauntingly beautiful 2015 album *All the Roads That Lead Us Home* and a wonderful collection of holiday songs that came out the next year. But after getting plucked out of the 6,000 or so applicants to the Tiny Desk Contest and having her music shared worldwide under the imprimatur of NPR, her artistic life has been advancing at a much more rapid clip.

After the run of shows she played in the wake of the Tiny Desk Contest, she and her husband, Paul, threw all their energy into maintaining this surge of momentum. They sold their home, quit their day jobs, and hit the road, with Lea playing shows all over North America and beyond. This year alone, she's made stops at The Decemberists-curated

Travelers Rest Festival in Missoula, Montana, and the Reykjavik Arts Festival in Iceland.

"It's a weird feeling because I don't know where songs come from," Lea admits. "I know I write them. But I do feel like the beginning of a song starts as a subconscious or superconscious idea. You don't really own it. So what is really cool and weird about playing for people you don't know is seeing people connect with an idea that you only feel partial ownership over."

Next Steps

Lea's most recent, and perhaps biggest, leap comes in the form of her new album, *Learning How to Stay*. Unlike previous solo efforts, which mixed a few original songs in with traditional folk tunes from the UK and Scandinavia, Lea wrote the majority of the material on this record herself. She also sings on nearly every tune, mixing her measured, yet quaint vocal tones with the plainspoken poetry of her lyrics. It's an affecting combination that plants deep her messages on the power of art and imagination ("Dark To Light And Dark Again"), self-reliance ("Lost In The Woods"), and the mosaic of emotions that is being in love.

Another change for Lea was the decision to welcome in a variety of other musicians to help flesh out the songs. The core ensemble is made up of a quartet of Minnesotan players including guitarists and co-producers Dave Mehling and Al Church, and drummer Martin Dosh, who used to perform with Andrew Bird. Throughout there are numerous guest appearances by Sparhawk; singer-songwriter Haley, who sings harmony vocals on three tracks; and The Cloak Ox member Jeremy Ylvisaker playing guitar on a handful of tunes. Even Bob Boilen joins in the fun, providing an array of sound effects on the dreamy "The Last Three Feet." The songs still fit in comfortably with the modern folk mood of Lea's previous work, only now her canvas feels bigger and more colorful.

"It some ways it feels like the next step," Lea says of *Learning How to Stay*'s sound. "But it came kind of out of necessity and just wanting to try something new. I don't have a lot of vocabulary for guitars, drums, and bass. I know what I like and I can say, 'I want it to sound like outer space,' but that's where my vocabulary drops off. I never thought of myself as a producer but I started realizing that I had all these ideas on how to produce songs. I think it's cool to know now that I can make my ideas work."

This new way of work also feels like an example of how Lea is still finding the right balance between complete self-reliance and conscientious collaboration. In terms of the latter, she managed to raise enough money through a crowdfunding campaign to pay for the majority of the recording and release of *Learning How to Stay*. She's also working with a UK label to release the album overseas. And although she still handles all the granular details of booking a tour, she recently hired an assistant to make the initial contact with venues.

Still, Lea maintains her resilient independence, often with a healthy sense of innovation. "I almost started working with a manager a couple of times, but then decided not to," Lea says. "I had a booking agent for a while. I do think it's cool to have support. But if you can do it, and you can manage it, you can make it happen in a really cool way. I'm sure there's some limitations to doing these things myself, but right now, I don't mind reinventing the wheel." ■

SHAWN STIGSELL

LITTLE SEEDS

Jeremy Dutcher moves Native songs from archives to modern ears

by Devon Legér

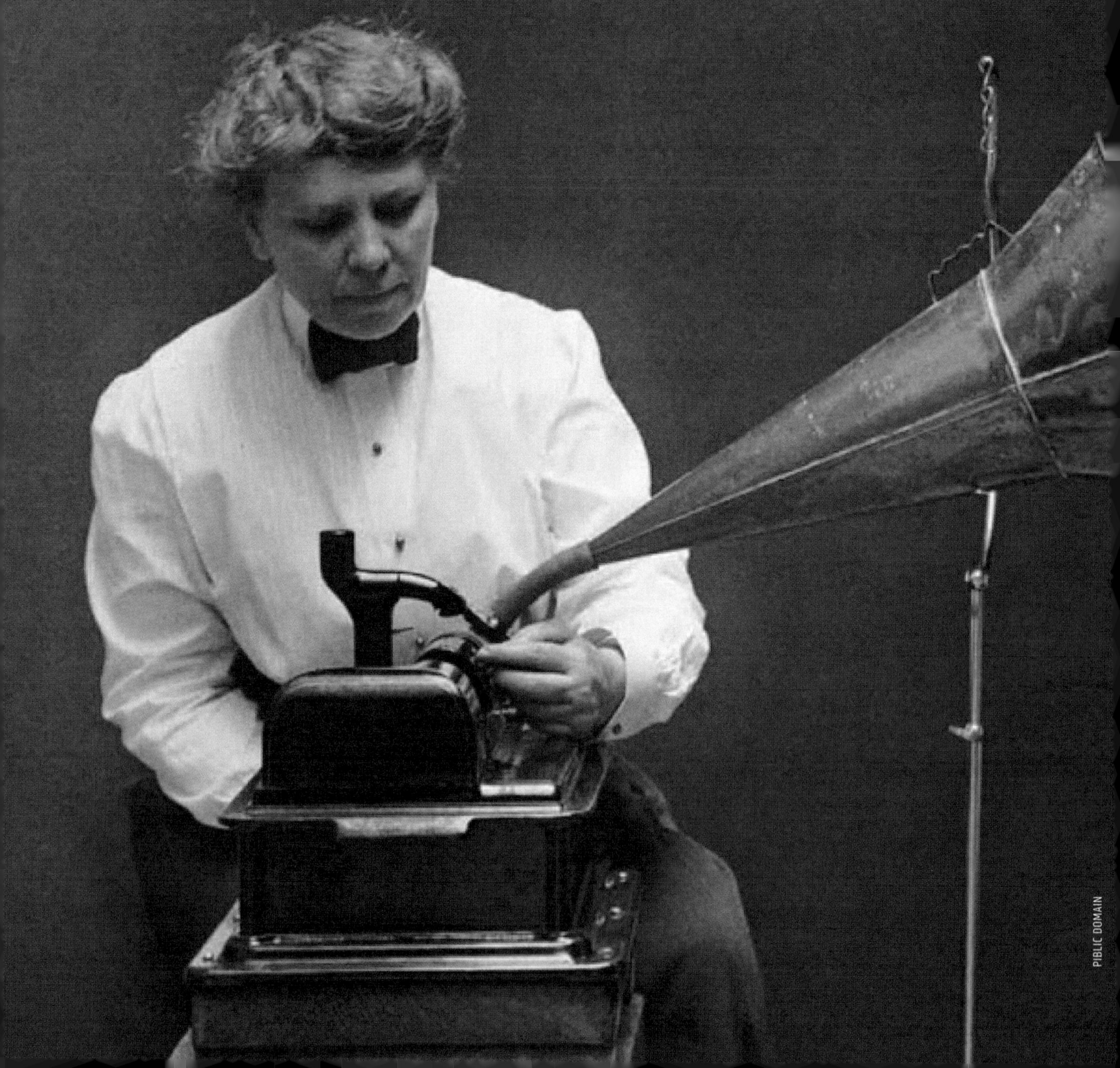

PUBLIC DOMAIN

Frances Densmore listening to wax cylinder phonograph with
Mountain Chief, a Blackfoot Indian, in 1916

THERE'S A FAMOUS OLD photograph that's come to represent the relationship between Native Americans and anthropologists. In this photo from 1916, the anthropologist Frances Densmore, a famous recordist and transcriber of Native music and culture, is bent over, fiddling with an old gramophone. To the right, Ninna-Stako, mountain chief of the Blackfoot Nation, stares hard at the horn of the gramophone, his ceremonial headdress cascading down his back as if the sound of the music is blowing the feathers like wind. The gramophone sits impassive in the middle, connecting two very different people with very different perspectives. This moment in time — as well as many moments captured in the field recordings anthropologists made of Native Americans during the early 1900s — are freeze-frames of the past, but they are not impassive.

Anthropologists brought powerful, even foreign, technology into often isolated communities and recorded through the lens of their own prejudices and perspectives. The original Native sources for these recordings saw through this and made their own choices about what to sing or present and how to frame it.

Jeremy Dutcher knows this story well. A trained operatic tenor and composer, Dutcher is a member of the Tobique First Nation in New Brunswick, Canada, and one of only 600 speakers of the Wolastoq language. For nearly 100 years, the Canadian government banned songs and other manifestations of the culture of the Wolastoqiyik (Maliseet people). But in the middle of that ban, and nine years before that fateful photograph of Densmore and Ninna-Stako, the anthropologist William Mechling came to the Maliseet lands, home of the Wolastoqiyik. He lived among them for seven years, recording songs on Edison wax cylinders and ultimately creating some of the earliest recordings of indigenous people. Of the 100 recordings, only 75 have survived, the others broken, melted, or lost. The wax cylinders reside now in the Canadian Museum of Civilization in Ottawa, all that remain of the traditional songs of the Wolastoq people, a cultural legacy dating back thousands of years.

A few hours before his performance at the Vancouver Queer Arts Festival, Dutcher sits with me in a small public park in town. He's thinking now about the 25 songs that were lost. "I'll never hear those songs," he says. "That hurts a little. But so many of them weren't [lost]. I took those 75 and tried to understand them a little bit to embody them."

Dutcher discovered these recordings at the behest of a tribal elder, Maggie Paul. Having studied classical voice in college, Dutcher was looking for Native songs in the classical canon and coming up empty. Paul herself had been to the archives, but had only been able to learn one song. So she pushed him, just a little, to make the trip to Ottawa. "Our elders will do that," Dutcher says. "They'll drop little seeds. They won't pressure and they won't watch over you, but they'll plant a seed and they'll see where it goes." He impulsively sent off a quick email letting the archivists know he was coming, and then showed up in person to claim what was he saw as his right.

"That was the ethos of this project," Dutcher explains. "I'm not asking permission, I'm just taking it because they're ours. This material and these songs, they belong with the people they came from."

To their credit, the museum curators opened the doors wide, and Dutcher began a five-year process of translating these recordings into a more modern setting, all in the original language, culminating in his powerful debut album, *Wolastoqiyik Lintuwakonawa.* The album's a triumphant blend of Dutcher's classically trained vocals and the richness of the Wolastoq language, but mostly it's the melodies of these old songs, translated to Dutcher's piano and voice, that transport the listener.

"It became very obvious that the conversation that I was having at that moment with me and my ancestor was medicine and it was what was needed right now to create healing in our communities. Getting to sing along with that and being in conversation with that voice speaks to the cultural continuity of what was taken but not lost."

Jeremy Dutcher

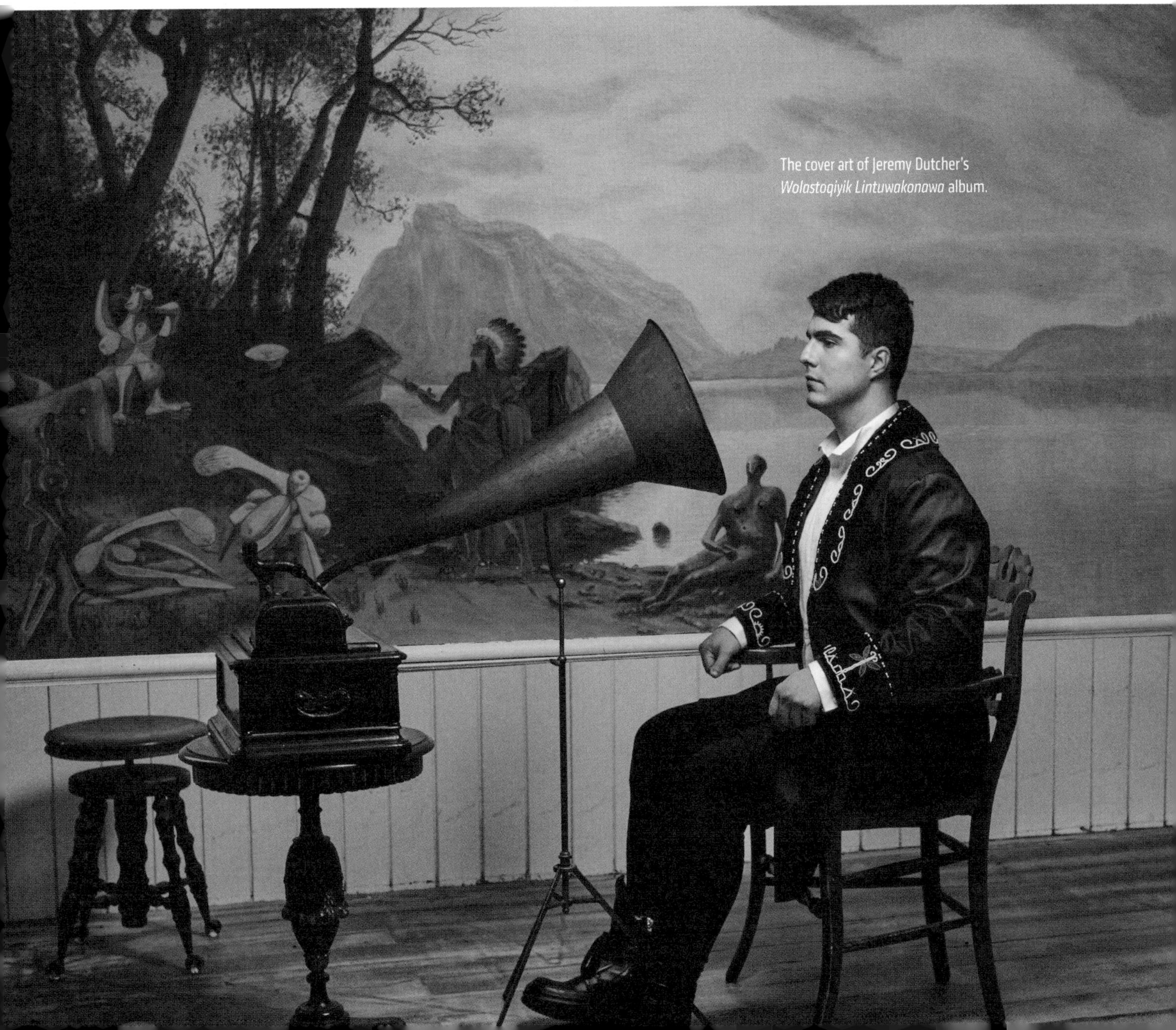

The cover art of Jeremy Dutcher's *Wolastoqiyik Lintuwakonawa* album.

Dutcher's been in heavy demand in Canada and beyond with these songs, and the album garnered critical acclaim, even winning Canada's prestigious Polaris Music Prize in 2018. But this warm reception exists in harsh contrast to the past acceptance of these same songs.

The forced assimilation of the Wolastoqiyik and many other tribes in Canada, the United States, and elsewhere in the world is a brutally tragic history, and that context makes listening to Dutcher's interpretations of music all the more strange and remarkable.

Dutcher laughs bitterly while talking about how Mechling arrived in the middle of this Canadian ban and set about legally recording that which was illegal: "These songs were collected in the early 1900s at a time when it was illegal, under Canadian law, for indigenous folks to practice ceremony, song, dance in public," he says. "Then all of a sudden this anthropologist comes along and says, 'Oh, you know that thing we've been telling you was illegal for 50 years already, could you just sing it for me? That would be great.' Then it was another 50 years until that law was repealed. Not until 1951."

Today, though the larger First Nations and Native culture of powwow drum and dance still exists among tribal members, the songs Mechling captured in wax are only rarely remembered. And, as Dutcher admits, there's very little, if any, modern music that has been written in the Wolastoq language.

Dutcher says he sees singing these songs today as a conversation between himself and his community. But it's more than that. It's also a direct conversation between himself and his ancestors whose voices have been captured on wax.

Performing that night at the Queer Arts Festival, Dutcher introduced his "ancestor player," an iPad that he used to play snippets from the wax cylinder recordings. These snippets played behind his expressive piano playing, or philosophized after he sang, or, in the most powerful moments of the performance, dueted with Dutcher's voice onstage.

Like other young artists using archival music in performance (like Appalachian-inspired folk duo Anna & Elizabeth), Dutcher hears more in the old recordings than just the music. "When you hear the voice, and you hear the melody [in the recordings], it's great, and you hear the crackle and it's lovely. But what you're actually hearing is the life. Sometimes you can hear them dancing in the background, or laughing, or talking over somebody who's singing, or telling jokes.

"In the first track of the record, 'Mehcinut,' it ends with a speech [the singer] gives about life and death and what happens after. There's something untranslatable in that. It just needs to be part of it." It's these moments of life that give breath to the songs, that push them beyond the simple wax they were originally carved in. "It was always very, very important to have [these

MATT BARNES

recordings] onstage," Dutcher says. "Now I'm bringing my ancestors wherever I go. They're traveling across the world. I was in Asia last year, Scandinavia. I'm going to Europe early next year."

A Conversation with Ancestors

Dutcher has a deep respect for these recordings, and a deep connection with them, but the work on his new album is compositionally his, and to create this he had to figure out how to meld his classical training with music that had been created thousands of years before the Western scale or tempos were imprinted on Native culture.

Additionally, classical music has not always been kind to traditional music. The anthropologist Densmore herself was known for forcing Native songs into the strict confines of classical notation and transcription. On first arriving at the archive, transcription was Dutcher's first way of trying to get the music out of the reel-to-reels that they'd been transferred to because wax cylinders degrade so quickly. Without a way to take the music home to listen in depth, he resorted to transcribing songs as fast as possible. As the songs were digitized into WAV files, he was finally able to take them home to spend time with these voices in a more natural way. "I was in that deep process of listening over and over," he says. "Then I would sit at the piano. I would trace the outlines of these melodies, where they went, and then try to find ways to shape around them. I didn't sing them at all. It wasn't time for me to sing them yet."

When he did begin singing along with the songs, he says, "it became very obvious that the conversation that I was having at that moment with me and my ancestor was medicine and it was what was needed right now to create healing in our communities. Getting to sing along with that and being in conversation with that voice speaks to the cultural continuity of what was taken but not lost."

Dutcher pushes back hard against the idea that he's resurrecting anything with his music, even with only 75 songs and 600 native Wolastoq speakers left. "There's a lot of talk of sadness and what we've lost. For me, this is a celebration of the cultural continuity of our people. As Maggie Paul says, 'The circle was never broken. We never lost these things. They just had to go away for a little while to keep them safe. And now it's time to bring them out and show everyone how amazing it is.'"

Dutcher sees himself as a mirror, "collecting all of that cultural knowledge and information from the archive and then taking it back and singing into the community." In this way, he plays both sides of the famous Densmore and Ninna-Stako photograph, a photograph that's haunted him ever since he first saw it in college in an ethnomusicology class. For his album he commissioned two photographs, one for the front cover and one for the back cover. On the front, he's Ninna-Stako — the voice, the tradition, sitting stoically and staring into the depths of the gramophone horn. On the back, he's the field recorder, the anthropologist, the diligent student of the tradition.

In the end, he's come around to a positive perspective on the anthropologist that first recorded these songs. "Museums and anthropologists are not neutral. It's all politically framed and it's all through a lens of the context of the day. But I give a little prayer to Edison every day for that wax cylinder technology because it allowed me to do what I do and to connect with my ancestors in such a deeper way than I was able to before."

Dutcher says that it gives him great hope for where we're going because now the culture isn't going away. "It can't now," he says. "Now that we've been able to document and protect, now it's just about dissemination."

These sentiments echo the words of the original source of Dutcher's inspiration, Maggie Paul. Taken from his own field recording of Paul, his interview with her starts off the song "Eqpahak." "When you bring the songs back, you bring the dances back," she says. "You can bring the people back. You can bring everything back." ■

NO DEPRESSION

Contributors

ALLISON HUSSEY is a North Carolina native whose favorite things include record shopping, critters, biscuits, folklore, and social justice. She now lives in Durham, North Carolina, and is the music editor at INDY Week, with other work appearing at Pitchfork, Bandcamp, Noisey, and The Bluegrass Situation.

ANNA ROBERTS-GEVALT learned fiddle and banjo from a generous community in Eastern Kentucky. She currently lives in Brooklyn, New York, where she works as one half of Anna & Elizabeth, makes videos, and plays experimental music.

BEVERLY BRYAN is a writer and former editor of MTV Iggy. Her articles about music have been published in Paste, Remezcla, Noisey, and SPIN. She co-hosts a podcast about Latin American indie music called Songmess and resides in Brooklyn, New York.

BONNIE STIERNBERG is a freelance writer based in Brooklyn, New York, by way of Chicago, covering music, television and pop culture. She was formerly music editor at Paste, and recently her work has appeared in Billboard and Rolling Stone.

CAITLIN MCDONAGH is a Canadian visual artist and illustrator. Her work is inspired by folklore, storytelling, symbolism, and the natural world. She resides in Montreal, where her days are filled with coffee, music, her partner, and two cats.

CHRIS PARKER is a freelance journalist and author of *King James Brings The Land a Crown: The Definitive Tale of the Cavaliers' 2016 Title Run.* His eclectic writing has appeared in The Guardian, Billboard, Variety, The Daily Beast, and dozens of alt-weeklies. He resides in Cleveland, where he mostly tries to avoid thinking bad thoughts.

CRAIG HAVIGHURST is a writer and broadcaster who oversees music news and talk at WMOT-FM in Nashville. He's producer and host of *The String*, a talk and features show/podcast about American music. He's also a founding co-host and producer of Music City Roots.

DEVON LÉGER is a music publicist and freelance music journalist, writing about and interviewing roots musicians in the US and abroad with a focus on marginalized artists in the folk community. Devon also researches Acadian fiddle traditions, an interest from his own heritage, and has been traveling back to the Maritime provinces to find and record elder fiddlers.

DREW CHRISTIE is a Seattle-based animator and illustrator. His work has been featured by The New York Times, Huffington Post, The Atlantic, and others.

GREG CAHILL is a San Francisco Bay Area writer. He is the former editor of Acoustic Guitar magazine and once listened for 10 minutes while Ramblin' Jack Elliott described his favorite milkshake (it's all about the viscosity).

HILARY SAUNDERS is the managing editor at *No Depression* and her previous work has appeared in Paste, ESPN, Next City, The Jewish Daily Forward, and more. She's a proud alumna of the University of Miami and a firm believer that rock and roll can save the world.

KIM RUEHL was an editor of *No Depression* from 2008 to 2017, bringing the magazine back into print in 2015 and ending her run as editor-in-chief. She has also written for Billboard, NPR, Yes Magazine, and others. She is working on a book about labor and civil rights organizer and folk song collector Zilphia Horton, to be published by the University of Texas Press. She lives in Asheville, North Carolina, with her wife.

MATT POWELL has written for *No Depression*, Emmys.com, Angels Flight • literary west, and Humor in America. He is a founding member of Los Angeles-based roots trio Dago Red Revival.

MARCUS AMAKER is Charleston, South Carolina's first poet laureate and an award-winning graphic designer. His poetry has been featured on PBS Newshour, TEDxCharleston, Alaska Airwaves magazine, and more. His latest book, *empath,* is also an album collaboration with Grammy-nominated musician/producer Quentin E. Baxter of Ranky Tanky.

ROBERT HAM's writing has been featured in Billboard, Pitchfork, Paste, and Stereogum. He lives quite happily with his wife, son, and four rambunctious cats in Portland, Oregon. Follow him on Twitter at @roberthamwriter.

SCOTT NURKIN is a musician and visual artist who plays drums for Birds of Avalon and Dynamite Brothers. He paints murals for a living through his company The Mural Shop and his favorite record of all time is ZZ Top's *Tejas.*

STACY CHANDLER is the assistant editor for *No Depression.* She is a freelance journalist living in Raleigh, North Carolina, with her husband, their daughter, a big dumb yellow dog, a fiddle, and a stack of half-finished embroidery projects.

THOMAS GRANT RICHARDSON is an independent folklorist and ethnomusicologist based in Santa Fe, New Mexico. He has worked as a fieldworker/consultant for the traditional arts agencies of New Mexico, Utah, Oregon, Missouri, Minnesota, and Iowa. He's been learning to play the banjo for 10 years.

TIM EASTON is a traveling songwriter and proprietor of Campfire Propaganda Records & Books. He currently lives just outside Nashville in Whites Creek, Tennessee.

WILL HODGE is an Atlanta-based journalist who has contributed to Rolling Stone, Paste, CMT Edge, and various other outlets. He is also the editor and community manager for NoiseTrade. When he's not writing about the folk music foundations of classic country and punk rock, he can be found daydreaming about the hip-hop/new wave sonic wonderland of late-'70s/early '80s New York City.

MARK SELIGER

Screen Door

AN OCEAN OF POSSIBILITY

BY ANNA ROBERTS-GEVALT

For the third Anna & Elizabeth album, *The Invisible Comes to Us,* which came out last spring, we recorded 10 ballads gleaned from two years of archival research. My bandmate Elizabeth LaPrelle and I reached into the same group of traditional songs that experimenters like Aaron Copland, Bill Monroe, and others did before us. But we latched onto a particular thread within this kind of music to drive our own experiments — the stories. We want to share how music can come out of a specific time and place and into everyday life.

On stage, especially, we've tried to find ways to fuse stories and sounds, context and melodies. We've tried movement, sewing, and painting. We've used scrolling illustrations called crankies as well as puppets, radio dramas, and film. But with this record, we experimented most with sound itself.

Here's a story of one such experiment from *The Invisible Comes to Us.*

I found one of the songs on the record in an old book by Carrie Grover at the American Folklife Center in Washington, DC. In a note, Grover recalled her family's last night in Nova Scotia before they immigrated to Maine in the 1890s, when she was a young girl. They had a goodbye party; her mother was asked to sing "Farewell to Erin," an old Irish song about immigration. She begins to sing, Grover writes, "but her voice broke, and she had to leave the room. I never heard her sing it again."

The story brought me, for a fleeting moment, out of the archive and into that room. What a visceral pain lodged in a song!

I brought the song to Elizabeth and we agreed that we wanted to sit with that feeling and not let it pass so easily. We also wanted to try to bring that pain into the rooms we were performing in.

Around this time, I'd started listening to experimental drone music — snippets of Ellen Fullman, Henry Flynt, and others. Its insistence drew me in — slow moving clouds of sound that hit me heavily and reminded me sonically of a bagpipe's drone. But these experimenters invited new possibilities and permissions for me — harshness, patience, and new textures I hadn't listened for before.

Drone music felt like a landscape to us. It reminded us of the ocean, with its single, unchanging horizon. It was like a way in to imagining ourselves in Grover's situation, on a ship and leaving our homes.

On *The Invisible Comes to Us,* we brought in experimental pedal steel player Susan Alcorn to play "Farewell to Erin" with us. She's a dear friend, one who coaxes a deep, harsh, beautiful sound out of her instrument, one who's been living in experimental zones for decades. In the studio, we told her the story of the song, and then, as Susan put it, "we entered the ocean." Elizabeth's singing felt more vulnerable than I'd ever heard her. Everything felt personal.

When we perform "Farewell to Erin" live, I play a single note on my fiddle, trying to channel that droning and stay in the feeling. We also have a painting to accompany the sound — a slow scrolling crankie made with 30 feet of unchanging ocean horizon to wind for the duration of the song. I remember feeling terrified during the first performance of the piece. *Did the audience get it?* I remember hearing them shifting in their seats. *Was this a terrible idea?*

Four excruciating minutes later, the ocean scene was over. An old man came up to me after that show and said, "I didn't really know what was happening — and then I realized nothing was happening. And then I thought, 'The ocean is so big.'"

Over the years since the initial experiment, the performance has grown deeper — as has my trust in it — as well as my acceptance that maybe not everyone will like it. I've started to hear new things in the fiddle, learned to be more patient, and lean into the harsh noises if that's what I, or Elizabeth, might feel that day. We mark our success by the days we feel the most present.

I experiment in search of these moments. There is a lot of exploring yet to do with traditional songs — taking them apart and putting them back together — in search of these feelings, these stories, these landscapes lodged within them. ■

HANNAH DEVEREUX